PATTERN
CUTTING
for Kids' Clothing

A RotoVision book

Published in 2014 by Search Press Ltd.
Wellwood, North Farm Road
Tunbridge Wells
Kent, TN2 3DR

This book is produced by
RotoVision SA
Sheridan House, 114 Western Road
Hove, BN3 1DD

ISBN 978-1-78221-028-3

Commissioning Editor: Isheeta Mustafi
Editor: Janice Pariat
Assistant Editor: Tamsin Richardson
Art Director: Lucy Smith
Art Editor: Jennifer Osborne
Design concept: Emily Portnoi
Layout: Rebecca Stephenson
Cover Design: Michelle Rowlandson

Image credits
Front cover (all photos): Clothing by Andrea Thomas-
Lambe of Thomas Parks Gifts, photography by Samantha
Provenzano of Puddle Jumpers Photography.
Back cover (L-R): Clothing by Carla Hegeman Crim and
Jennifer Paganelli of Sis Boom, photography by Emily
Korff of Veralana Photography; Clothing and photography
by M&Co.

PATTERN CUTTING
for Kids' Clothing

All you need to know about designing, adapting and customising sewing patterns for children's clothes

CARLA HEGEMAN CRIM

SEARCH PRESS

Contents

1 The Basics

2 Starting Points

3 Garments

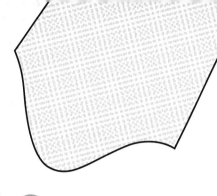

4

Going Pro

Clothing: Judy Buchanan of Hickity Pickity. Photography: Georgia Handy.

Introduction

In recent years, handmade children's clothing has become popular. This has inspired women (and a few men) to take up sewing, not only for their own children, but also for home-based businesses. As a result, the demand for 'boutique' patterns has exploded. Unlike the typical tissue patterns of yesteryear, modern sewing patterns include detailed sewing instructions complete with colour diagrams and/or photographs. This is possible because of digital technology that allows for the creation and distribution of patterns in electronic format. Most boutique pattern company founders are mums who themselves started out sewing for children. Their backgrounds are diverse, and most have never taken a class in fashion design. What they do have in common is a willingness to experiment and learn.

This book is a great resource for those who are comfortable tackling most sewing patterns and are ready to branch out into making their own patterns. Instead of pages of complex formulas for drafting, you are given the basic building blocks that you can modify to make your own. Detailed size charts help show how a child's body grows and develops. Explanations of fit and pattern manipulation help to take all the mystery out of the modification process. Beautiful photographs, provided by boutique pattern makers, designers and home sewists of all levels, provide helpful inspiration.

Commonly used pattern abbreviations and annotations:

SA – Seam Allowance
CF – Centre Front
CB – Centre Back
WOF – Width of Fabric
RST – Right Sides Together
WST – Wrong Sides Together
RSO – Right Sides Out
WSO – Wrong Sides Out

Symbol	Description
Bent double-pointed arrow	Indicates placement of an edge on the fold of the fabric.
Double-pointed arrow	Shows how the pattern should be positioned relative to the grainline of the fabric.
Single-pointed arrow	Shows the direction of the nap in furry or fuzzy fabrics.
'I' shape	Buttonhole placement marking; may or may not show button placement with an x or a dot.
Dot	Can be used to show stitching stop and start points, or indicate a placement point.
Triangle	Indicates the position of a notch to be cut into (or outside of) the seam allowance for matching purposes.

Opposite and this page top: Clothing: Andrea Thomas-Lambe of Thomas Parks Gifts. Photography: Samantha Provenzano of Puddle Jumpers Photography. **This page bottom:** Clothing: Courtney Chu of courtneycourtney. Photography: Angela Neil of Treasures for Tots.

How to use this book

This book includes 12 patterns and a pattern for a basic block that you can print, modify and use as per the instructions in this book.

Downloading the patterns

Scan the QR code at the top of the page with your smartphone or webcam attached to your computer (A). Note that you will need to have a QR code reader installed on your device. These readers are usually free to download. If you do not feel you can use the QR codes, simply type in the following address to your web browser:

http://www.rotovision.com/downloads/2383

Each pattern can be accessed by typing in the relevant page number at the end of the web address; so to access the pattern on page 28, you need to add the number 28 to the end of the web address: http://www.rotovision.com/downloads/2383/28 On the web page, you will see a button to download the pattern (B).

When joining the printed pages together to assemble the whole pattern, overlap and attach the pieces at the shaded area as shown (C).

Printing the patterns

The blocks are designed to be printed at 100 per cent. Before printing the patterns, make sure that page scaling is set to None in the Adobe Acrobat print window. To be sure that your blocks are going to print at the correct size, measure the box on the first page of each size group pattern pages. It should measure 2.5cm by 2.5cm (1in by 1in).

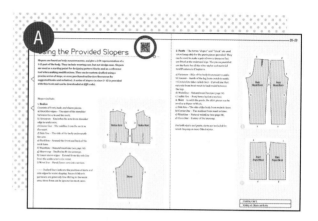

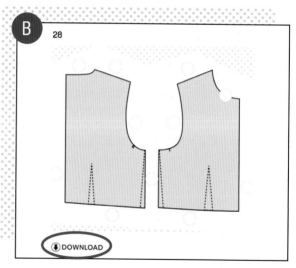

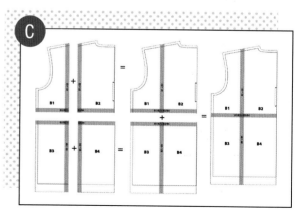

Using the patterns

Each pattern is graded in different sizes and the sizes appear on different pages of the pattern. If you only wish to print the sizes that are relevant to you, use the tables below as a guide:

Page 28: Basic blocks

Size	Page
4	1–10
6	11–22
8B	23–36
8G	37–50
10B	51–64
10G	65–78
12B	79–92
12G	93–106

Page 46: Peasant tops

Size	Page
3–4	1–12
5–6	13–24
7–8	25–36
9–10	37–50
11–12	51–64

Page 50: Casual shirt

Size	Page
3–4	1–15
5–6	16–29
7–8	30–46
9–10	47–63
11–12	64–80

Page 54: T-shirts

Size	Page
3–4	1–11
5–6	12–22
7–8	23–34
9–10	35–46
11–12	47–58

Page 60: Coats & jackets

Size	Page
3–4	1–19
5–6	20–38
7–8	39–59
9–10	60–80
11–12	81–101

Page 66: Waistcoats

Size	Page
3–4	1–6
5–6	7–14
7–8	15–22
9–10	23–30
11–12	31–38

Page 70: Tunic top

Size	Page
3–4	1–16
5–6	17–35
7–8	36–53
9–10	54–71
11–12	72–89

Page 74: Corsets & halters

Size	Page
3–4	1–4
5–6	5–8
7–8	9–14
9–10	15–22
11–12	23–30

Page 80: Basic Trousers

Size	Page
4	1–12
6	13–28
8B	29–44
8G	45–64
10B	65–84
10G	85–106
12B	107–130
12G	131–154

Page 96: Basic Skirts

Size	Page
3–4	1–8
5–6	9–20
7–8	21–32
9–10	33–44
11–12	45–56

Page 110: Basic Dresses

Size	Page
3–4	1–12
5–6	13–28
7–8	29–44
9–10	45–60
11–12	61–80

Page 116: Bodice dress

Size	Page
3–4	1–13
5–6	14–25
7–8	26–37
9–10	38–50
11–12	51–62

Page 128: Basic Playsuits

Size	Page
3–4	1–13
5–6	14–34
7–8	35–60
9–10	61–87
11–12	88–123

This page top: Clothing and photography: M&Co. This page bottom left and right: Clothing: Judy Buchanan of Hickity Pickity. Photography: Georgia Handy. Opposite: Clothing: Carla Hegeman Crim and Jennifer Paganelli of Sis Boom. Photography: Emily Korff, Veralana Photography.

Clothing: Judy Buchanan of Hickity Pickity. Photography: Georgia Handy.

Chapter I
Measurements

The first step to making well-fitting patterns is to have access to accurate, detailed size charts. There are many available online and in books. In 2002 the British Standards Institution (BSI) introduced new standards for clothing sizes, based on European guidelines. Although these provide common labelling standards, pattern companies and manufacturers have mostly continued to use their own charts, which they have developed based on older standards and customer preferences. UK sizes are generally based on a system introduced in the 1950s, which has evolved over time according to taste and changes in body shapes. Hip, waist and chest measurements tend to stay proportional, but labelling may vary. Up-to-date US charts are included in 'standards' – measurement sets based on large population studies, published by the American Society for Testing and Materials (ASTM). Earlier standards (in the public domain) run very close to the current standards for children's wear.

Charts based on public domain data appear on pages 16–17 – the size designations are in line with average sizes for each age group. Use these charts as is, or as a starting point for developing your own sizing metrics. As designer, you can shift sizes or modify proportions to fit a certain body type better.

Measuring techniques

Body measurements

Body (also called girth) measurements are taken around certain landmark points. For younger children, boys and girls have similar measurements and proportions. At about size 7, girls will show a slimming of the waist and a broadening of the hips relative to the chest. Boys, however, stay relatively proportional throughout the chest and hips, with a less dramatic tapering at the waist. Therefore, separate charts are provided. Note: In the past, 6x was a standard size in between 6 and 7. In recent years, 6x is seen less and less, and brands bridge the gap by making 6 a little bigger and 7 a bit smaller.

The charts include the following body measurements:

Chest – Measured at the widest point, under the armpits and including the tips of the shoulder blades.

Waist – Measured at the narrowest point, or at the bend in the waist for children with tummies. An old trick is to tie a string around the middle, and let the child do some toe-touches. The string will settle at the natural waistline.

Hip – Measured near the top of the hipbone; includes the top of the buttocks. Usually the widest point, but can vary from child to child.

Thigh – Measured around the upper leg at the widest point.

Ankle – Measured at the bony projection just above the foot.

Upper arm – Measured at the widest point between the shoulder and the elbow.

Wrist – Measured at the bony projection just above the hand.

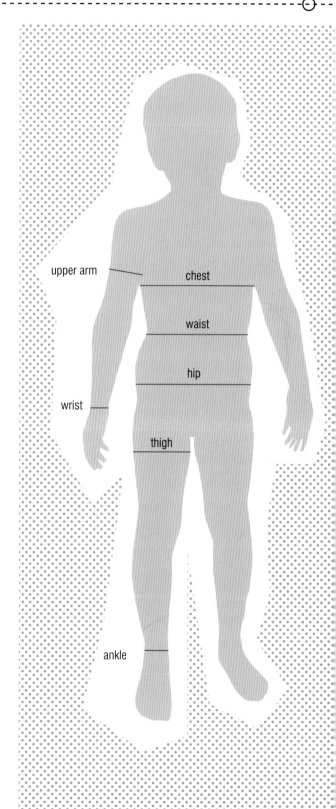

Vertical measurements

These are the landmarks that answer the question 'How long should I make it?' For example, shoulder to knee is a classic dress length, and shoulder to hip is a good top length. Crotch to ankle (or floor, depending on the style) is synonymous with inseam. Though a standard age/size is provided, vertical measurements can be considered separate from body type. For example, two 109cm (43in) tall children will have vertical landmarks at the same position, even if one measures for a 4 and the other measures for a 6 girth-wise. Separate charts are provided for older boys and girls. While landmarks will fall in the same place for a given height with structure, age/size designations are different, with girls being taller for any given size.

The charts include the following body measurements:

Crown – Positioned at the top of the head.

Shoulder – Positioned at the centre of the shoulder, between the arm and neck. It is at the same level as the bottom cervical vertebra, a prominent bone at the back of the neck. For describing garment lengths, the shoulder is a much more useful term since neckline position varies.

Waist, hip, ankle and wrist – See body measurements on page 14.

Crotch – Positioned at the leg/torso intersection.

Ankle – See body measurements on page 14.

Elbow – Positioned at the bend in the arm.

Wrist – See body measurements on page 14.

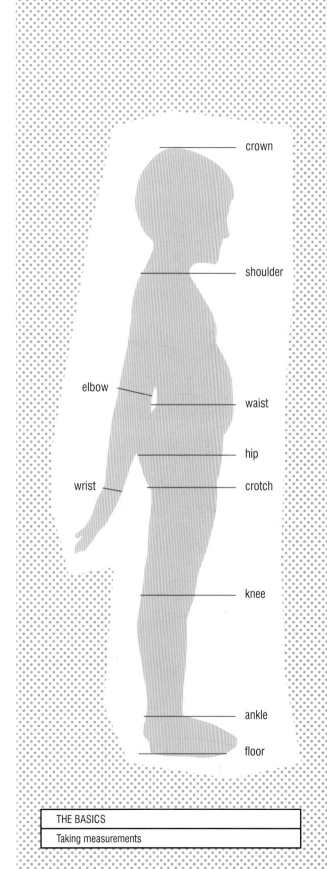

THE BASICS

Taking measurements

Size Charts

Body measurements

Younger girls and boys

Approximate age/size	3	4	5	6	6x/7
average height	94cm	101.6cm	109.2cm	116.8cm	121.9cm
chest	55.9cm	58.4cm	61cm	63.5cm	64.8cm
waist	53.3cm	54.6cm	55.9cm	57.2cm	58.4cm
hip	57.2cm	59.7cm	62.2cm	64.8cm	67.3cm
upper arm	16.2cm	16.9cm	17.2cm	17.8cm	18.4cm
thigh	31.8cm	33cm	34.3cm	35.6cm	36.8cm
wrist	10.8cm	11.4cm	11.8cm	12.1cm	12.4cm
ankle	14.6cm	14.9cm	15.6cm	15.9cm	16.5cm

Older boys

Approximate age/size	7	8	9	10	11	12
average height	121.9cm	127cm	132.1cm	137.2cm	142.2cm	147.3cm
chest	65.4cm	67.3cm	69.2cm	71.1cm	73cm	74.9cm
waist	58.4cm	59.7cm	61cm	62.2cm	63.5cm	64.8cm
hip	65.4cm	67.3cm	69.2cm	71.1cm	73.7cm	76.2cm
upper arm	17.8cm	18.4cm	19.1cm	19.7cm	20.3cm	21cm
thigh	36.5cm	38.1cm	39.7cm	41cm	42.2cm	43.5cm
wrist	12.4cm	12.7cm	13cm	13.3cm	13.3cm	14.3cm
ankle	16.5cm	17.2cm	17.8cm	18.4cm	18.4cm	19.4cm

Older girls

Approximate age/size	7	8	9	10	11	12
average height	129.5cm	134.6cm	138.4cm	139.7cm	142.9cm	146.1cm
chest	66cm	68.6cm	70.5cm	72.4cm	74.3cm	76.2cm
waist	57.2cm	58.4cm	59.7cm	61cm	62.2cm	63.5cm
hip	69.9cm	72.4cm	74.3cm	76.2cm	78.7cm	81.3cm
upper arm	18.8cm	19.7cm	20.3cm	20.7cm	21cm	21.6cm
thigh	40cm	41.6cm	42.6cm	43.8cm	45.1cm	46.7cm
wrist	12.4cm	12.7cm	13cm	13.3cm	13.3cm	14.3cm
ankle	16.5cm	17.2cm	17.8cm	18.4cm	18.4cm	19.4cm

Vertical measurements

Younger girls and boys

Approximate age/size	3	4	5	6	6x/7
height	94cm	101.6cm	109.2cm	116.8cm	121.9cm
shoulder to wrist	28.6cm	34.6cm	38.1cm	41cm	43.5cm
shoulder to elbow	19.7cm	22.9cm	25.1cm	27cm	28.3cm
shoulder to waist	22.9cm	24.1cm	25.4cm	26.7cm	27.3cm
shoulder to hip	36.8cm	38.1cm	40cm	42.6cm	43.2cm
shoulder to crotch	38.4cm	41cm	43.5cm	46.1cm	47.3cm
shoulder to knee	52.1cm	56.5cm	61cm	65.4cm	68.6cm
shoulder to ankle	71.5cm	77.8cm	84.5cm	91.1cm	95.6cm
shoulder to floor	76.2cm	83.2cm	90.2cm	97.2cm	101.6cm
waist to crotch	16.8cm	18.1cm	19.4cm	20cm	20.6cm
waist to knee	30.5cm	33.6cm	36.8cm	39.4cm	41.9cm
waist to ankle	49.9cm	54.9cm	60.3cm	65.1cm	68.9cm
waist to floor	54.6cm	60.3cm	66cm	71.1cm	74.9cm
hip to floor	39.4cm	45.1cm	50.2cm	54.6cm	58.4cm
crotch to knee	13.7cm	15.6cm	17.5cm	19.4cm	21.3cm
crotch to ankle	33cm	36.8cm	41cm	45.1cm	48.3cm
crotch to floor	37.8cm	42.2cm	46.7cm	51.1cm	54.3cm
knee to floor	24.1cm	26.7cm	29.2cm	31.8cm	33cm
ankle to floor	4.8cm	5.4cm	5.7cm	6cm	6cm

Older boys

Approximate age/size	8	9	10	12
height	127cm	132cm	137cm	147cm
shoulder to wrist	45.1cm	47.4cm	49.5cm	54cm
shoulder to elbow	29.5cm	30.8cm	32.2cm	34.9cm
shoulder to waist	25.4cm	26cm	27cm	28.6cm
shoulder to hip	42.2cm	43.2cm	45cm	47.3cm
shoulder to crotch	49.2cm	50.8cm	52.4cm	55.6cm
shoulder to knee	71.5cm	74.6cm	77.8cm	85.7cm
shoulder to ankle	99.7cm	104cm	109cm	118cm
shoulder to floor	106cm	110cm	115cm	125cm
waist to crotch	22.2cm	22.9cm	23.5cm	24.8cm
waist to knee	44.5cm	46.7cm	48.9cm	54.9cm
waist to ankle	72.7cm	76.5cm	80cm	87.6cm
waist to floor	78.7cm	82.6cm	86.4cm	94cm
hip to floor	63.5cm	67.3cm	70.5cm	77.5cm
crotch to knee	22.2cm	23.8cm	25.4cm	30.1cm
crotch to ankle	50.5cm	53.6cm	56.5cm	62.9cm
crotch to floor	56.5cm	59.7cm	62.9cm	69.2cm
knee to floor	34.3cm	35.9cm	37.5cm	39cm
ankle to floor	6cm	6cm	6.4cm	6.4cm

Older girls

Approximate age/size	7	8	10	12
height	129cm	135cm	140cm	146cm
shoulder to wrist	45.7cm	48cm	50.2cm	52.7cm
shoulder to elbow	29.7cm	31.1cm	32.5cm	34.1cm
shoulder to waist	25.4cm	26.4cm	27.3cm	28.3cm
shoulder to hip	42.5cm	43.2cm	44.5cm	46.4cm
shoulder to crotch	49.9cm	51.8cm	53.6cm	56.2cm
shoulder to knee	65.1cm	75.9cm	79.1cm	82.9cm
shoulder to ankle	102cm	107cm	111cm	117cm
shoulder to floor	108cm	113cm	113cm	124cm
waist to crotch	22.5cm	23.8cm	25.1cm	26.3cm
waist to knee	45.4cm	48cm	50.5cm	53cm
waist to ankle	74.9cm	79.1cm	82.9cm	87.3cm
waist to floor	81.3cm	85.4cm	89.5cm	94cm
hip to floor	66cm	70.2cm	73.7cm	77.5cm
crotch to knee	22.9cm	24cm	25.4cm	26.7cm
crotch to ankle	52.4cm	55.2cm	57.8cm	61cm
crotch to floor	58.8cm	61.6cm	64.5cm	67.6cm
knee to floor	35.9cm	37.5cm	39cm	41cm
ankle to floor	6.4cm	6.4cm	6.7cm	6.7cm

Clothing: Judy Buchanan of Hickity Pickity. Photography: Georgia Handy.

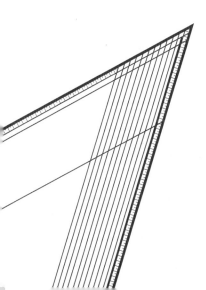

Chapter 2
Finishes, fasteners and fit considerations

In the world of fashion, the designer determines the final look of the garment, imparting his or her unique flair and style. Sketches of the 'silhouette' are then passed on to the pattern cutter, who incorporates construction details and makes a series of patterns to fit a range of sizes. As designer and pattern cutter, you have complete control over the style, finishing and fit of the garment. If you will be selling the pattern, it is important to make the construction as simple and elegant as possible. From your own sewing experience, you undoubtedly have preferences and little 'tricks' for getting great results.

Finishes and fasteners

Finishes

When designing a garment, some of the biggest decisions involve finishing the interior seams and outer edges.

For interior seams, the most popular and efficient finish is overlocking. This can be done using sewing machine stitches or an overlocker. From a pattern-cutting perspective, 0.6cm (¼in) is ample seam allowance for overlocking. For couture finishes like French and Hong Kong seams, a larger allowance of 1.2cm–1.5cm (½–⅝in) is needed. In addition, if you want the option of altering the finished product to a larger size, larger seam allowances are necessary. Just try to keep in mind that smaller allowances are preferable from a fabric consumption perspective.

Hems – Arm and leg openings are often finished with hems. For a single-folded hem, the garment is first edge-finished, then folded to the appropriate hem allowance and stitched. For a double-folded hem, the raw edge is folded, and then a second fold is made to encase the raw edge prior to stitching. The two folds added together equal the hem allowance.

Facings – Facings may be used to finish curved edges like necklines and sleeveless armholes (see page 71). Facings are stitched to the garment and turned to the opposite side, enclosing the raw edges. Interfacing may be added to give needed stability to the garment opening.

Bias binding – Bias binding may be used to finish curved edges or hems without the need for additional pattern pieces. Single-fold tape shows on one side of the garment; double-sided tape shows on both the inner and outer side of the garment.

Linings – Linings are duplicates of pattern pieces that finish curved edges and enclose interior seams. A garment may be fully or partially lined.

Casings – Casings are constructed like hems but contain either elastic or a drawstring to cinch in the fabric.

Fasteners

The choice of fastener depends on the style of garment and the age of the child (see pages 22—23). Another consideration is how difficult the fastener is to install. If the pattern is intended for beginners, it is best to stick with fastener-free elasticised styles or a button/loop closure. Snaps or press studs (both sew-on and press-on) are also good, simple options. For more intermediate patterns, buttonholes can be used. For both snaps and buttons/buttonholes, overlapping plackets or tabs must be included. For those more advanced at sewing, a zip is a clean fastener option that requires little modification to the pattern (a 1.5cm [⅝in] seam allowance is sufficient for most zips).

Photography: Sherry Heck.

Clothing considerations

Like grown-ups, kids come in all shapes and sizes. Because they lack significant curves, it is much easier to draft patterns for children than for women. Comfort is of the essence for children's clothing. Adults may be willing to suffer for fashion, but children will have nothing to do with anything that is tight, itchy or bulky.

Ease

Ease, or tolerance, is a term used to describe the difference in size between a garment and the person wearing it. A woven garment with no ease would fit like a second skin with no room for movement. Wearing ease is the amount of ease necessary to make a garment wearable (tight, but wearable). Design ease is the amount of ease beyond wearing ease that gives the garment a shape and style. Different parts of a garment can have different amounts of design ease. For example, the basic bodice dress (page 116) is fitted at the chest and waist, but loose-fitting at the hips.

	Close-fitting (wearing ease only)	Fitted	Semi-fitted	Loose-fitting
Chest	5cm (2in)	6.5–10cm (2½–4in)	10–12cm (4–5in)	12cm (5in)+
Waist	1.2cm (½in)	2.5–5cm (1–2in)	5–7.5cm (2–3in)	7.5cm (3in)+
Hips	5cm (2in)	6.5–7.5cm (2½–3in)	7.5–10cm (3–4in)	10cm (4in)+

This chart provides general ease recommendations for tops, bottoms, dresses and playsuits made of woven fabrics. Note: jackets and coats require at least an extra 2.5cm (1in) of ease to accommodate the garment(s) beneath.

Body type

As children grow, their proportions change and they develop differently according to gender. Even within a size group, there can be differences in proportions. In the garment industry, children are classified as slim, regular and husky/plus size. For a given height, slims have a smaller chest/hip girth than regulars, and huskies/plus size have a larger chest/hip girth than regulars. The proportions differ as well. Slims have more tapered waists, while huskies have more of a tummy. To make a garment work for a wide range of body types (without lots of adjustment on the end user's part), it is best to offer fit flexibility as much as the style allows. For example, trousers with wide hips and an elasticised waist are more likely to fit slims, regulars and huskies than fitted trousers with a zip and no elastic. For girls, A-line and empire dress styles are great because they are only fitted in the chest area, so waist and hip measurements are less important.

Growth

Children grow so fast and they undergo growth spurts that make it seem as if they have changed sizes overnight. The most noticeable growth is vertical. Trousers that are centimetres too short may fit fine at the waist. For years, sewing mums have used tricks to extend the life of kids' clothes. For example, deeper hems can be let out to accommodate growth. For trousers, adding cuffs is another great option. As far as girth goes, elastic saves the day once again. Buttonhole elastic, which has become popular with retailers in recent years, is a great invention that allows for more fitted waistband styles to be drawn in and let out without any alteration of the garment.

Durability

Children's play clothes need to be rugged and washable. Material choice plays a large role in durability, but stitching is important too. Seams should always be finished to prevent fraying and, ultimately, splitting. Reinforcement stitching can be added to parts of the garment that experience lots of movement and strain, like crotches and underarms. For dress clothes that will be worn only for special occasions, fabric durability is less of a concern, but proper stitching techniques should be used so the garment can be handed down from generation to generation as a treasured heirloom.

Many little girls love to dress up in frilly confections every day, and not just on special occasions. To get the best of both worlds, design formal outfits to be made with durable, breathable cottons.

Self-dressing

Keep the age and independence level of the child in mind when designing. Make sure the garment is suited to independent potty breaks and quick changes due to accidents. Fasteners in particular can make a big difference. Back buttons and zips can be difficult for a child (or an adult, for that matter) to manipulate. For younger children, elastic is always a good bet for trousers. To get the look of dress trousers, consider making a flat front with a mock fly and an elasticised back. With dresses, the fasteners are not as much of a concern as far as the toilet is concerned. Playsuits, however, need to have easy, accessible fasteners.

Safety

Retail clothing manufacturers must adhere to safety standards. Choking hazards are of particular concern. Long straps and ties are not recommended for small children, as they can wrap around the neck. Drawstrings in necklines and hoods should be avoided for all ages, as they can get caught and cause constriction. Before designing patterns, familiarise yourself with current standards so that the end user can create safe, compliant garments (see page 150).

Clothing: Judy Buchanan of Hickity Pickity.
Photography: Georgia Handy.

This page: Clothing and photography: M&Co. Opposite: Clothing: Judy Buchanan of Hickity Pickity.
Photography: Georgia Handy.

Clothing: Andrea Thomas-Lambe of Thomas Parks Gifts. Photography: Samantha Provenzano of Puddle Jumpers Photography.

Chapter 3
Working with blocks

Blocks are great foundations for drafting and manipulating patterns. Basic blocks – also called fitting shells, or slopers – are skin-tight patterns that act as a 2D tailor's dummy. You could sew a garment from a basic block, but it would be quite uncomfortable (and the child would outgrow it immediately), so these are then revised so that the necessary comfort and some degree of style is worked into the design. In this book, both basic and revised blocks are provided to give you a jump-start on your pattern range. Laying the revised block atop the original gives you a sense of the fit and is a basis for making stylistic modifications.

Using the provided blocks

Blocks are based on body measurements and give a 2D representation
of a 3D part of the body. They include wearing ease, but not design ease.
Basic blocks are used as a starting point for designing pattern blocks and as
a reference tool when making modifications. They can be custom-drafted
using a precise series of steps, or even purchased online (see Resources for
suggested books and websites). A series of blocks in sizes 3–12 (see page 16)
is provided with this book and can be downloaded as described on page 8.

Blocks include:

1. Bodice
Consists of front, back and sleeve pieces.
a) Shoulder edges – Span the shoulder between the
arm and the neck.
b) Armholes – Encircle the arm from shoulder
edge to underarm.
c) Centre line – The midline from the neck to
the waist.
d) Side line – The side of the body underneath
the arm.
e) Neckline – Around the front and back of the
neck base.
f) Waistline – Natural waistline (see page 14).
g) Sleeve crown – Drafted to fit the armhole.
h) Inner sleeve edges – Extend from the side line from
the underarm to the wrist.
i) Wrist line – Hand/lower arm intersection.

------ Dashed lines indicate the position of darts
and side edges for waist shaping. Since children's
garments are generally free-fitting in the waist
area, these lines can be ignored in most cases.

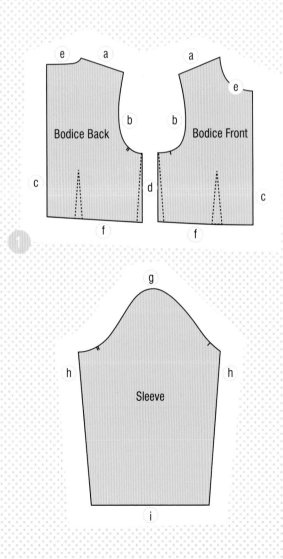

2. Trousers – The trouser blocks provided can be used as a basic block or a modified block. The pieces can be used to make a pair of woven trousers that are fitted at the waist and hips. These pieces are the basis for all the other styles and material modifications in Chapter 6.

a) Side seam – Side of the body from waist to ankle.
b) Inseam – Inside of the leg from crotch to ankle.
c) Crotch line (also called rise) – Curved line that extends from front waist to back waist between the legs.
d) Waistline – Natural waistline (see page 14).
e) Ankle line – Foot/lower leg intersection.

3. Skirt – As with the trousers, the skirt pieces can be used as a basic or modified block.
a) Side line – The side of the body from waist to knee.
b) Centre line – The midline from waist to knee.
c) Waistline – Natural waistline (see page 14).
d) Knee line – Centre of the kneecap.

For both skirts and trousers, darts are included for waist shaping on more fitted styles.

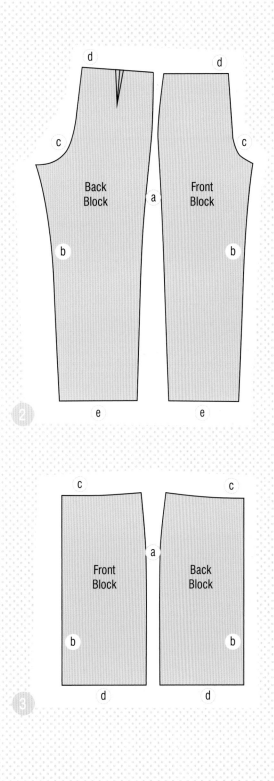

STARTING POINTS

Working with blocks

Using and modifying basic blocks

Modified blocks are the most basic of sewing patterns. Unlike basic blocks, they have the design ease necessary to give a garment a specific shape. As the name suggests, pattern blocks are used to 'build' new designs. The blocks are provided in sets. For example, the T-shirt set includes a front bodice block, a back bodice block and a sleeve block. Many garment types can be derived from a single set of blocks. For example, the T-shirt block set is only a few minor modifications away from being a sweatshirt, jacket or waistcoat pattern. In Section 3, instructions are given to make an entire wardrobe from the provided blocks.

Traditionally, seam and hem allowances are not included in blocks. This allows the designer the flexibility to modify the seams and add the desired allowances. The digital blocks provided offer the best of both worlds. The basic block pattern has a solid outline, and the dashed line surrounding the block pattern represents suggested seam and hem allowances for sewing directly from the unmodified block (1). If minor changes are made to the block, it is quite easy to adjust the seam allowance accordingly (2).

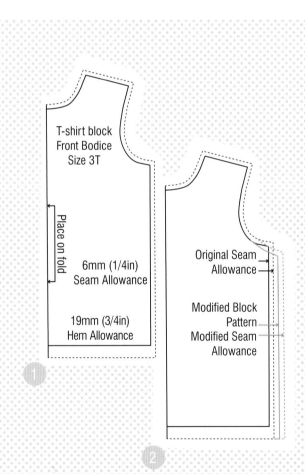

T-shirt block
Front Bodice
Size 3T

Place on fold

6mm (1/4in)
Seam Allowance

19mm (3/4in)
Hem Allowance

Original Seam
Allowance

Modified Block
Pattern
Modified Seam
Allowance

When modifying a block, the corresponding basic block can be used as a reference tool. Like a 2D tailor's dummy, the basic block indicates how a garment made from it will fit the body. Figure 3 shows a modified front tunic block superimposed on the basic front bodice block. With the centre lines and shoulders aligned, the basic block gives a good indication of neckline position and overall ease. The darts in the basic block show where the body curves. Since most of the garments in this book are free-fitting (and children are relatively cylindrical), the darts are not shown unless relevant to the design.

As with any sewing project, it is a good idea to first make a test garment out of inexpensive fabric to work out design issues and confirm proper sizing. Such samples are often referred to as toiles, or muslins. For best results, make your toiles using materials that are similar to the intended final fashion fabric with regards to weave and fibre composition.

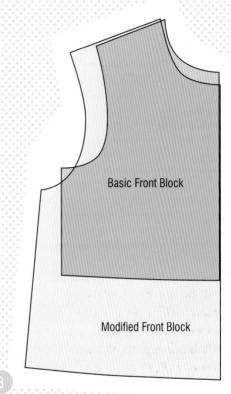

Basic Front Block

Modified Front Block

3

TIP

Blocks can be printed on durable card stock and used again and again. For blocks that will be modified, use vellum or inexpensive recycled paper. When stacked, the basic block will show through the relatively transparent modified block pattern.

STARTING POINTS
Working with blocks

Clothing: Judy Buchanan of Hickity Pickity. Photography: Georgia Handy.

Chapter 4
Altering patterns and making patterns from clothing

'It's all been done' is a line that comes up often in fashion. As mentioned in Chapter 10, the laws that apply to pattern modification are somewhat murky. For extremely unique designs, the equivalent of patents can be filed, and the designer is protected against infringement. When it comes to basic styles, however, the purpose is considered utilitarian, and previous designs are fair game with significant modifications. With that being said, actual pattern pieces or sewing instructions should not be copied; it is best to use the drafting and modification principles outlined in this book. The required tools are inexpensive and easy to use, so you can be up and running with the professionals in no time.

Drafting tools

Essential tools needed to draft and modify patterns include:

Clear ruler – Used to draw and square off straight lines. If you sew, it is likely that you already own one of these for rotary cutting. A ruler that is 60 x 15cm (24 x 6in) is a good size for drafting children's clothing. For longer trousers and dresses, a metre rule or yardstick is useful.

Measuring tape – Used to measure girth. Can also be turned on its edge and used to measure curved lines in the absence of a flexible ruler.

Paper – To print digital patterns, A4 paper is required. Wide paper like wrapping paper or newsprint is good for drafting new patterns or extending existing patterns. Thin pattern paper or tissue paper is good for tracing. Card stock is great for printing off blocks that will be used again and again.

French curve – Allows for smooth transition when drawing or modifying curved edges.

Other tools that are notessential but are helpful include:

Flexible ruler – Used to measure curved edges.

Tailor's dummy(s) – Used for test-fitting and creating patterns by draping. If you have the space and the resources, it is nice to have them in a range of sizes. If you can have only one, choose a medium size, so patterns made from it can be graded into smaller and larger sizes (see page 141).

Yardstick compass – For drawing large circles.

This page and opposite: Photography: Sherry Heck.

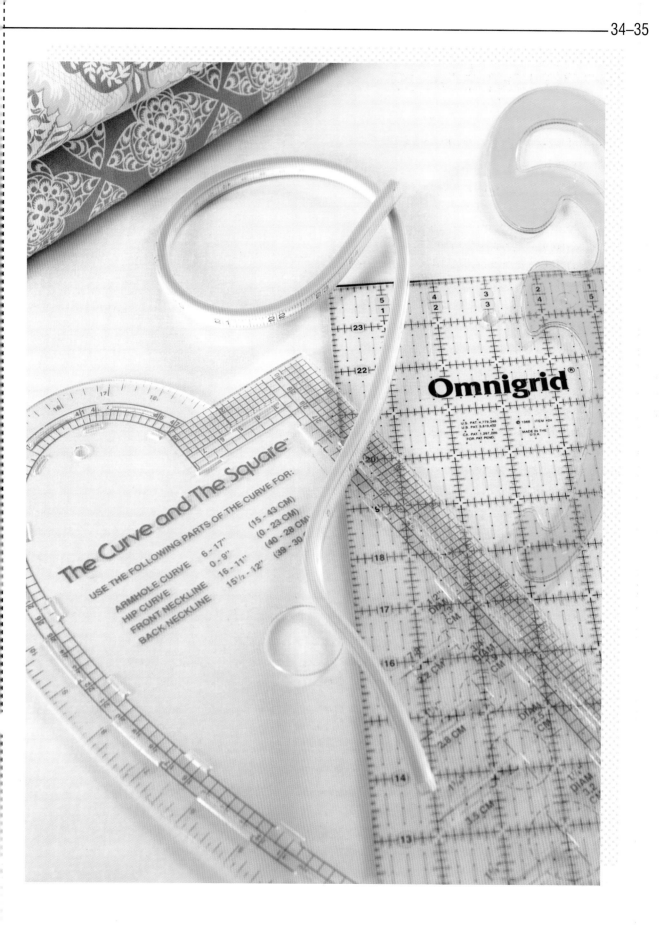

Modifying blocks

Lengthening and shortening

A pattern can be changed vertically to modify the style or the fit. This is very useful for accommodating different body types or fit preferences.

1. For very basic patterns with straight side edges, length modification is just a matter of moving the bottom line up or down by the desired amount.

To alter length without changing the overall shape, the pattern can be cut and reassembled. The cutting line can be at a single position, or multiple cutting lines can be used to increase length throughout the pattern. As children's clothes are fairly free-fitting, one cut line is generally sufficient for lengthening.

Typical horizontal cut line positions:

Sleeve – elbow level (a)

Shirt – waist level (b)

Trousers – knee level (c)

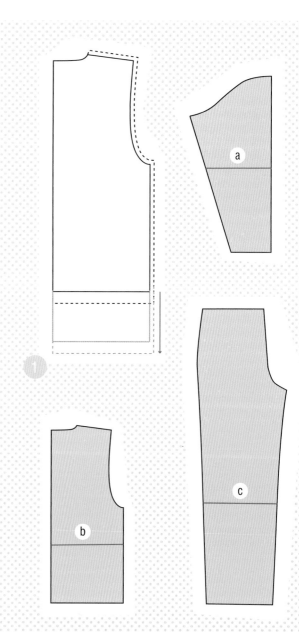

2. To lengthen: Draw a cut line at the desired position (a). Cut and spread the pattern sections apart by the desired distance (b), then use backing paper to bridge the gap(s).

3. To shorten: Overlap the sections and tape them together.

4. To lengthen in a specific area but maintain overall length: Lengthen at the desired position (a). Shorten by making an equal-sized overlap at a different cut line (b).

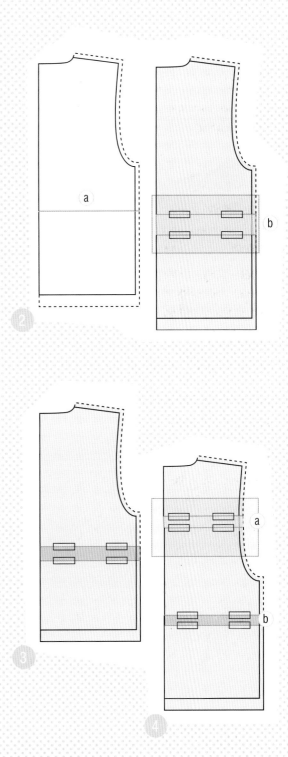

NOTE

Vertical or horizontal changes made on the front bodice should be repeated at the corresponding position on the back bodice.

STARTING POINTS

Altering patterns and making patterns from clothing

Adding fullness

Many of the block manipulations described in this book involve the addition of design ease, or tolerance, to one or more areas of a garment. This changes the overall shape and style. As described for length, the pattern is cut into sections and manipulated into a new width. The cuts are made lengthwise, however, and the sections can be moved to a fixed distance or angle.

Altering the cut (1)

By slashing and spreading pieces, girth is increased. The position of the cut greatly impacts the design.

Bodices/Shirts – to keep a dress or top pattern true to size, avoid adding volume to the neckline area (unless it will be gathered back to the original size, as seen on peasant tops). Adding volume in the shoulder area will make the edge of the armhole hang over the shoulder for a more relaxed fit (a). Note: For more fitted styles, the bottom armhole should be dropped to compensate for the lower position on the arm. Girth can also be increased by making the cut through the armhole, several centimetres from the side seam (b). For sleeved patterns, the sleeve should be expanded to fit the bodice (c).

Bodices can also be slashed horizontally, and fullness added to only the section below the line (see the yoke dress on page 122).

NOTE

For paper drafting, place the slashed pieces atop a large piece of paper. Tape the pieces into place in the desired position, then trace and connect the outer edges.

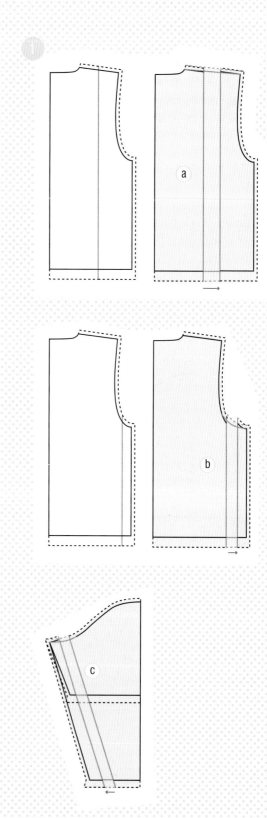

Trousers and skirts – Fullness can be added by cutting from the waistband to the bottom line (see page 84). Note: The resulting fuller style will then need to be cinched in by gathering and attaching to a waistband, or by adding a casing and elastic.

Adding flare (2)

Pattern pieces can be cut and sections angled to add flare. This makes for a smooth transition from narrow top to wider bottom. The degree of flare is up to the designer. A protractor is very useful for measuring angles so that the flare can be consistent from one section to the other, and from front to back. After the sections are rotated, they are reconnected with a smooth curve.

Skirts and dresses can be manipulated into A-line shapes by adding flare (see pages 98 and 114). Trousers can be flared by slashing and spreading below the desired point on the leg (see page 85).

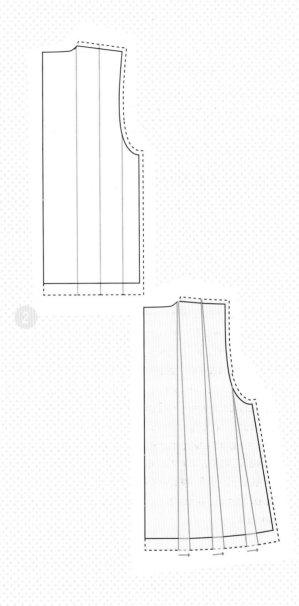

Clothing and photography: Sara Upshaw of Molly Blossom Designs.

Mixing patterns

Sometimes, the quickest and easiest way to get a desired look is to combine the best parts of two or more favourite patterns.

Mash-ups

A popular thing to do is take elements of one pattern and attach them to another. It is easiest to do with patterns from a single designer because they usually use the same size charts for all their patterns. However, mash-ups can be done with most patterns within a similar size range.

Dress mash-ups are very easy, especially with gathered skirts. Just make sure to make any skirt-length modifications needed to get the desired final dress length.

Sleeve mash-ups are also possible if the armholes are similar (especially for gathered sleeves that have a bit of wiggle room). If not, overlay the two patterns, and transfer the armhole from the pattern that came with the sleeve that will be used.

Frankenpatterns – Frankenpatterning involves actually merging two patterns together. The key is to line up vertical landmarks (waistline, hipline) and the centre line. For example, a button-up shirt pattern can be placed on an A-line pattern, and the edges can be connected to make an adorable shirtdress (see page 111).

Making patterns from existing clothing

A great way to get inspired is to take clothes off the rack and find out how they are drafted and put together. In fact, garage sales and charity shops are loaded with adorable, unique styles just begging to be made into patterns. Do not worry; knock-offs are commonplace in the world of fashion, and you will no doubt be modifying to make the design your own.

The non-destructive method is called rub-off pattern cutting. For simple garments, just fold the item in half lengthwise (wrong side facing out) and trace the seams. To prevent moving and shifting during the process, pin the item to a sheet of paper. The item will need to be traced from different positions, possibly even in small sections, to get an accurate representation.

For small children's garments, unless there is an emotional attachment to the item, it is best to take the item apart using an unpicker. Each individual piece can be traced or even put on a scanner (larger pieces may take multiple passes). Make note of the seam allowances and how the garment is assembled. If you are very motivated, you can sew the garment back together after creating the pattern.

Clothing: Andrea Thomas-Lambe of Thomas Parks Gifts. Photography: Samantha Provenzano of Puddle Jumpers Photography.

This page and opposite: Clothing: Andrea Thomas-Lambe of Thomas Parks Gifts. Photography: Samantha Provenzano of Puddle Jumpers Photography.

3 Garments

Clothing and photography: Debenhams.

Chapter 5
Tops

In children's sizes, shirts require little fabric, and the options are endless. For boys, casual shirts and T-shirts are staples. For girls, the same options are available — and then some! Add frills and fluff to make feminine blouses. Most top styles can easily be extended into dresses (see pages 110–113). Jackets and coats are derivatives of shirts that are designed to be worn as an outer layer. Again, the design options and functionalities are unlimited.

Peasant tops

Despite the humble name, peasant tops rule the world of boutique children's clothes. They are easy to sew and can be whipped up quickly, and the possibilities for customisation are limitless. With elasticised openings and big, roomy cuts, peasant tops are comfortable and free-fitting, making sizing easier for the designer. While cute and casual, they can be made to look more formal with the addition of ruffles, shirring and other adornments. Peasant tops are also perfect for layering. Combine one with a jumper dress (page 124) and ruffled trousers (page 89) for a complete ensemble. They are also a great foundation for a princess costume (see page 105).

In this basic peasant block, the front and back bodice pieces are identical. This allows for quick fabric cutting and easy sleeve attachment. Once the elastic is added, the armholes draw in towards the centres (indicated by the broken lines). The neckline falls near the collarbone, but it can be raised or lowered simply by adjusting the elastic length. The sleeve is cut on the fold, as both sides are the same.

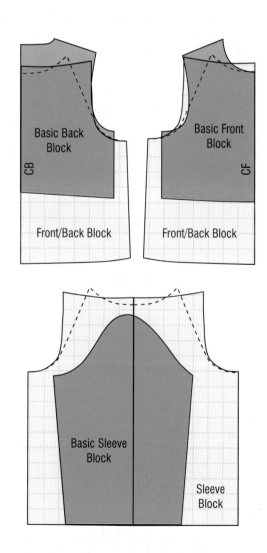

This page: Clothing and photography: Stacey Mann of Hailey Bugs Closet. **Opposite:** Clothing: Carla Hegeman Crim of Scientific Seamstress. Photography: Mari Hodge of Mari H Photography

Adjusting sleeve length

The full-length sleeve block (1) is just over wrist length on a child of average height for the given size. The arm opening can be raised for three-quarter, short or cap sleeves. As the sleeve covers most of the shoulder, the shoulder length must be included in the total length of the sleeve. For a short sleeve that falls 2.5cm (1in) above the elbow (2), add the shoulder length to the shoulder-to-elbow length, and subtract 2.5cm (1in). Make the arm opening line this distance from the top neckline edge. Add the casing or hem fold length as described on page 20, and then mark the cutting line (indicated by the broken line). For cap sleeves (3), it is necessary to drop the arm opening line under the arm slightly to accommodate the casing or hem folds. Calculate the length and then draw the upper line (a). Draw the lower line 2.5cm (1in) below the armhole (b). Connect the lines with a smooth S-shaped curve (c), and draw the cutting line parallel to the curve (d).

With elastic in the arm opening, peasant sleeves are puffed. Without elastic, longer peasant sleeves are bell-shaped, and shorter sleeves have a flared 'angel wing' look.

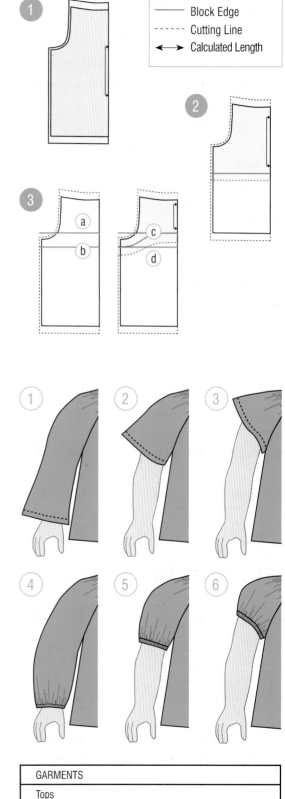

GARMENTS
Tops

Sleeveless and flutter sleeve options

A simple, popular variation of the peasant top is the pillowcase dress (1). The sleeves are eliminated, and the arm openings are finished with a facing that is drafted from the front/back block. Ribbons are strung through the front and back casings and tied at the shoulders. For the flutter sleeve option (2), the bottom edge of the sleeve is placed near the centre of the armhole, parallel to the top neckline edge. An armhole facing is drafted as described for the tunic on page 71.

Increasing fullness

Since the peasant top is gathered at the neckline, it naturally flares at the base, even though the block has a relatively straight cut. The centre lines can be moved further away from the side lines for fuller sleeves and front/back (3). This will increase the material in the piece, making for tighter gathers and an overall wider garment. However, this technique has limitations, as it can lead to a bulky chest area. To increase the fullness at the base (4), but not at the top, slash (a) and spread (b) on the front/back block to give an A-line shape, as described on page 114.

TIP

TIP

Thin fabrics like batiste and gingham can be gathered to a high degree of fullness, creating a light, flowing garment.

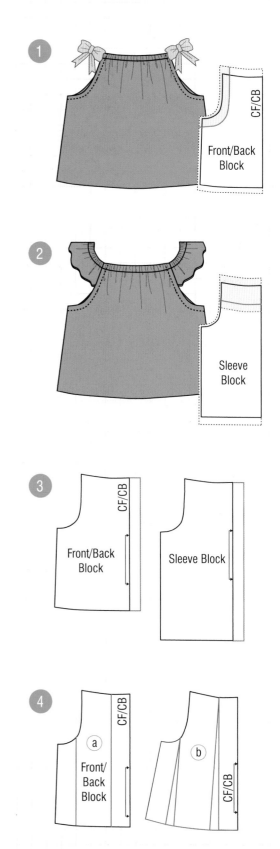

Adding fit control

The peasant top can be made to nip in and fit close to the body at various points on the bodice and sleeves. For this, the most commonly used technique is shirring (lines of stitching with elastic in the bobbin). Shirring can be placed just below the armholes for an empire style (1). It can also be placed at the natural waist (2), or near the bottom edge for a 'bubble top' look (3). Placed above the elbow, shirring gives sleeves a bohemian flair (4). Elastic may be used as an alternative to shirring. It can be stretched and stitched directly on to the fabric, or drawn through casings made from single-fold bias binding.

Top length and finishing options

This peasant block is designed to fall mid-thigh, but can be lengthened or shortened by moving the bottom hemline (see page 37). In general, garment length is measured from shoulder to hem, but since the shoulder is part of the sleeve piece, it is easier to measure the front/back piece from the centre neckline to hem (since the neckline is at shoulder level, the shoulder measurements in the chart may be used for length determination). Length can also be increased by the addition of ruffles (see pages 102—104).

Clothing and Photography: Breanne Crawford.

Casual shirt

This versatile style goes from casual to dress-up depending on the choice of fabrics and design options. It is a popular pattern for boys and a really great way to showcase fun fabrics and cute embellishments. Elements like pockets, epaulettes and side vents may be added for visual detail.

These blocks make for a casual shirt with a relaxed fit that is both comfortable and stylish. The shirt front can easily be folded to make a self-placket for buttons/buttonholes or snaps. Alternatively, a facing can be created for the centre front (see page 61). The back is the same width as the front and has the same armhole shape. The sleeve is cut on the fold, as both sides are the same. The shoulder seams fall slightly below shoulder level on the arm. The bottom of the sleeve is designed to fall around the elbow, but this can easily be adjusted. The sleeves can also be extended to full length to create a comfortable pyjama shirt.

A basic collar pattern is included with the shirt blocks. Both collar pieces (upper collar and under collar) are cut from this pattern. The collar is designed to meet in the centre when the shirt is buttoned. To draft custom collars, see pages 62–63.

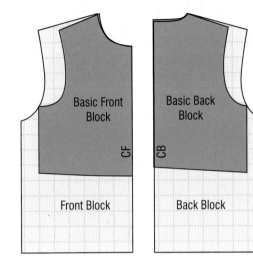

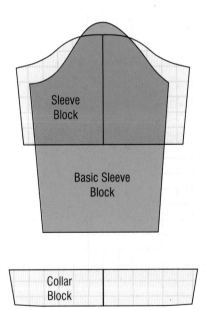

TIP

If you want to colour-block both the front and back of the shirt, consider doing vertical on one side and horizontal on the other. That way, you will not have to worry about matching the seams at the shoulders.

Colour blocking

With their boxy cut, casual shirts are excellent candidates for colour blocking. The pattern is cut in half, thirds or even quarters so that the piece can be constructed from multiple fabrics. This technique can be applied to the front and/or back for a retro bowling-shirt look. The width and placement of the blocks is up to the designer.

Draw one or more lines to divide the shirt into sections (a). For vertical colour blocking (1), the lines should run parallel to the centre line, while for horizontal colour blocking (2), the lines should run perpendicular. Cut the pattern at the lines (b). Add seam allowances (c).

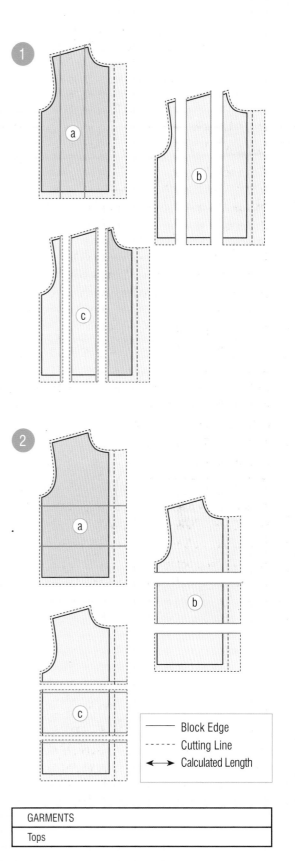

	Block Edge
-----	Cutting Line
◄───►	Calculated Length

GARMENTS
Tops

Clothing and photography: M&Co.

Pockets

Size and shape (1)

The bottom edge of the pocket can be straight (a),
pointed (b), curved (c) or squared off (d). The top
edge of the pocket is generally self-faced with a
straight or pointed extension. Additionally, pockets
can have a single pleat (e), double pleats (f), a flap
closure (g) or a decorative band (h). Shirt pockets
are usually slightly larger in height than width and
should be large enough for the wearer's hand to slip
inside. Oversized pockets give a fun look and are
perfect for storing treasures. For the best results,
'audition' shapes cut to the desired size on the front
block piece.

Pattern drafting (2)

After the pocket is drawn to the finished shape and
size (a), the self-facing is added to the top edge (b).
The hem allowance, generally 0.6cm (¼in), is
then added (c).

Placement (3)

Draw a top placement line that extends from the
centre front line to the armhole (a). Draw a second
line through the centre of the first line (b). Place
the top of the pocket block (without allowances or
facings) at the top placement line, and centre it
over the second line (c). Trace.

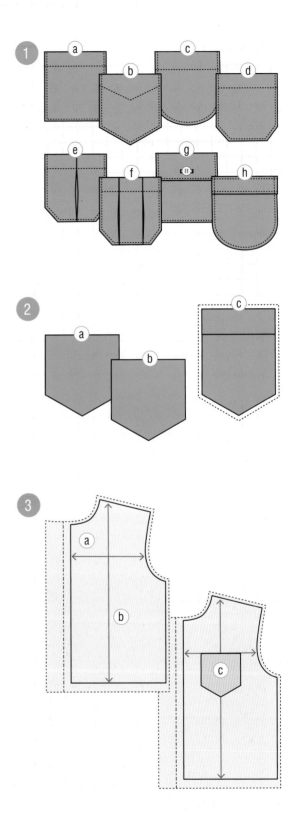

Epaulettes (1)

Epaulettes are faux or working button tabs sewn into the sleeve seam at the position of the shoulder seam. To draft an epaulette, first measure the shirt block at the shoulder edge (a). Draw a rectangle or pentagon that is three-quarters the length of the shoulder measurement and 2.5–4cm (1–1½in) wide (b). Add the seam allowance (c). Epaulettes can also be added to secure folds on mock or real sleeve cuffs. Draft as described above, but make them slightly longer than twice the cuff depth.

Bottom finish options (2)

The bottom edge may be modified into a curved shirt-tail shape. Drop the bottom edge at the centre front, and connect it to the side line at the original position with a gentle curve (a). Repeat for the back piece, which should be slightly longer than the front (b). Add the hem allowance (c).

Although not necessary for movement, vents may be added for style to the side seams at the bottom edges. The open vent edges can be finished with single or double folds. Modify the seam allowance to make tabs of the desired length and width (d).

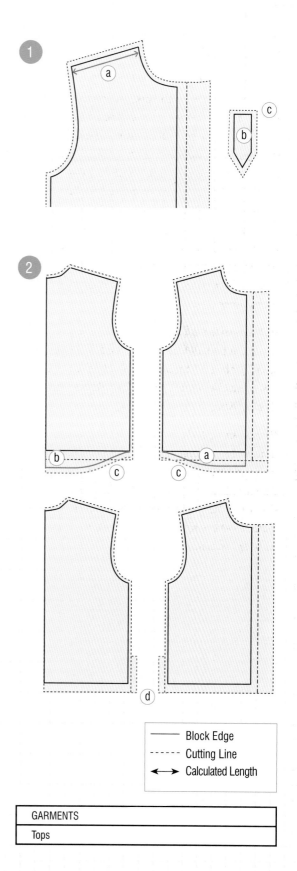

Clothing and photography: M&Co.

	Block Edge
	Cutting Line
	Calculated Length

GARMENTS
Tops

T-shirts

The T-shirt is a comfortable, durable and easily washable wardrobe staple for boys and girls alike. From a basic undershirt to a decked-out hoodie, this single pattern has numerous options. It is also wonderful for 'upcycling' existing T-shirts into custom creations.

This block has a basic fit that is trim but does not hug the body. The armholes are the same in the front and back, and they are dropped to a level that is appropriate for both boys and girls. The block neckline closely follows the basic block neckline, but will actually expand a little when worn, due to the stretchy nature of knits. Since the front and back armholes are the same, the sleeve is a mirror image and is cut on a fold. There are separate cutting lines provided for long and short sleeves, as the latter is slightly more tapered. Note that the long sleeve block is shorter than the full-length basic block. This compensates for lengthening due to stretching, and the finished garment will fall at wrist level on a child of the given height.

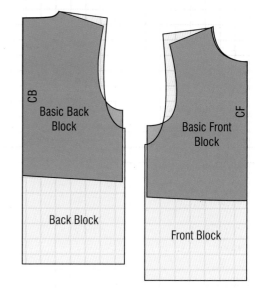

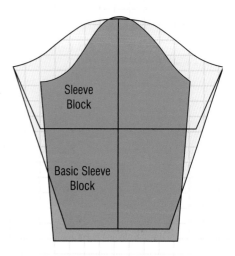

Clothing and photography: Dana White of Silly Jillybeans.

Fit modification

The fit of the basic T-shirt block is easy to alter. The slim-fit modification is great for rib-knit pyjamas and girls' tops. The loose-fit modification is perfect for hooded pullovers and layering over other shirts.

Slim fit (1)

For both the front and back blocks: Move the side seam edge in 1.2cm (½in) towards the centre (a). Move the armhole up 1.2cm (½in), relative to the original position, at the bottom corner (b). Redraw the armhole curve (c). Add the seam allowance (d). For the sleeve, move the side seam edge in 1.2cm (½in) towards the centre (e). Redraw the seam allowance (f).

Loose fit (2)

For both the front and back blocks: Move the side seam edge out 1.2cm (½in) towards the centre (a). Move the armhole down 1.2cm (½in), relative to the original position, at the bottom corner (b). Redraw the armhole curve (c). Add on the seam allowance (d). For the sleeve, move the side seam edge out 1.2cm (½in) towards the centre (e). Redraw the seam allowance (f).

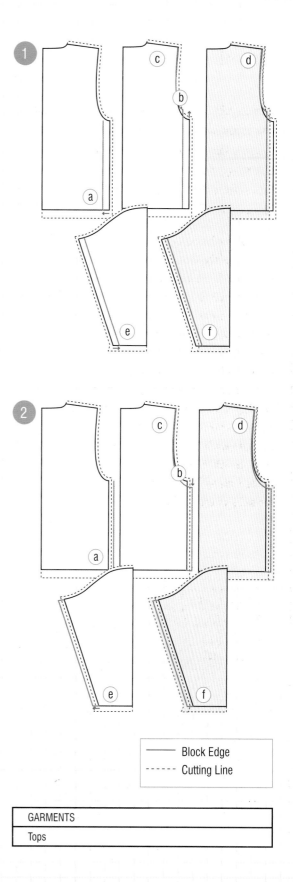

——	Block Edge
- - - -	Cutting Line

GARMENTS
Tops

Raglan sleeve

In this sporty variation of the classic T-shirt, the sleeve extends to the neckline and the shoulder seams are eliminated, making for easy sewing.

Front/Back (1)

On the back block: Draw a slightly curved line that connects the neckline to the armhole at the desired seam position (a). On a separate piece of paper, trace the shoulder section created by the new line. Make a reference mark at the intersection of the shoulder and armhole edges (b). Add the seam allowance (c). Trace the seam line on to the front block and add the seam allowance (d).

Sleeve (2)

Match the marked corner of the shoulder piece tracing with the centre top of the sleeve block (a). Arrange the shoulder piece so the tip is touching the sleeve block edge, and mark this position with an 'x' (b). Rotate the shoulder piece so that it is in line with the centre line of the sleeve block (c). Trace the shoulder edge (d). Redraw the neckline edge so that it is the same length, but make the curve a little smoother so that it fits with both the front and back blocks (e). Draw a line that connects the 'x' to the free end of the neckline edge (f). Add in the seam allowance (g).

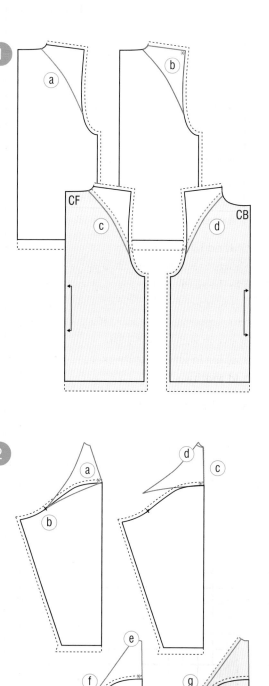

Sleeve modifications

Length (1)

The sleeve can be modified to fall higher or lower on the arm. For a three-quarter sleeve, the bottom edge will fall between the long- and short-sleeve cutting line (a). Make sure you taper the side line accordingly (b), and ensure the hem allowance kicks out a bit at the bottom edge so that it will fold neatly (c).

Cuff addition (2)

Shorten the sleeve by the finished cuff depth, and add the seam allowance (a). Draft the cuff piece so it is double the desired finished depth and about three-quarters the size of the bottom edge of the sleeve in width (b). Add the seam allowances, keeping in mind that the piece will be cut on a fold widthwise (c).

Mock layered sleeve (3)

Extend the short-sleeve cutting line over to the side edge for the long-sleeve version (a). Draw the hem allowance, making sure it kicks out a bit for neat folding (b). For the bottom part of the pattern, add the seam allowance above the short-sleeve cutting line (c).

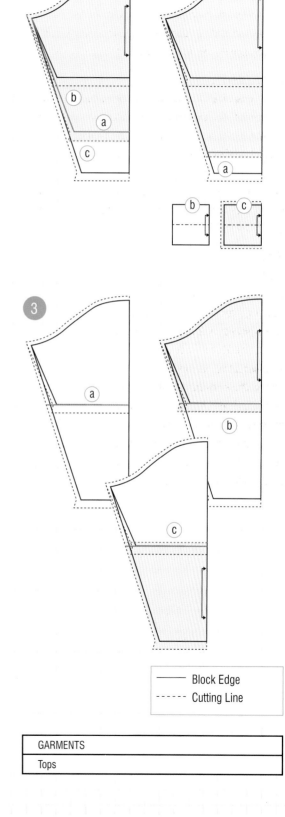

Clothing and photography: M&Co.

	Block Edge
	Cutting Line

GARMENTS
Tops

Neckline modifications

The depth and shape of the neckline can easily be modified. Scoops and V-necks are popular variations (see page 117).

The neckline may be finished by binding with ribbing or with fold-over elastic (1). In that case, no modification to the neckline is required. The binding should be cut to the same size or slightly shorter than the neckline (a).

For an attached neckband (2), move the front and back neckline down the finished ribbing depth, and then add the seam allowance (a). Draft the neckband piece so it is double the desired finished depth and about three-quarters the size of the neckline. Add the seam allowances (b).

For a mock or full-length turtleneck (3), move the front and back neckline down about 0.6cm (¼ in), and add the seam allowance (a). Draft the neckband piece so it is double the desired finished depth and about three-quarters the size of the neckline. Add the seam allowances (b).

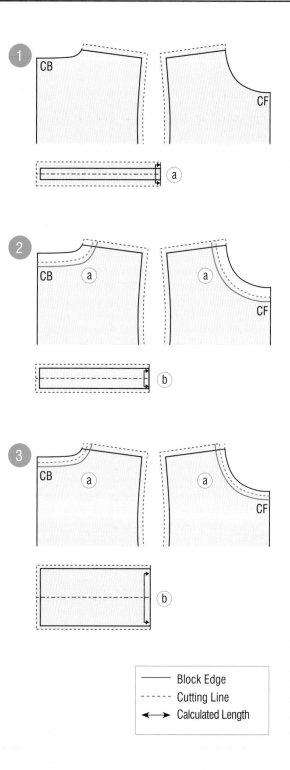

TIP

For cuff and neckband patterns, the size of the starting piece depends on the stretchiness of the fabric. Rib knits and Lycra blends are ideal because of their high stretch percentage. Less stretchy knits may be used, but the pieces will need to be longer.

——— Block Edge
- - - - - Cutting Line
←——→ Calculated Length

Hoods

Drafting (1)

a) Measure the back neckline (x) and front neckline (y).

b) Draw a line the length of x. Make a mark, and extend the line by the length of y.

c) Make parallel lines 2.5cm (1in) above and 2.5cm (1in) below the line. Draw a smooth curve that connects the ends of the lines and flexes at the mark between x and y.

d) z = the head to shoulder measurement + 5cm (2in) (see page 15; subtract shoulder to floor measurement from total height). Make a box with a base at y that is the length of z.

e) Draw a box on the left identical to the first (y x z).

f) Divide this box in half widthwise. Draw a smooth curve in the top corner of the top half.

g) Connect the top corner of the bottom half to the free end of the top parallel line.

h) Eliminate the parallel lines and the divided boxes. This leaves the basic hood block.

i) Add hem and seam allowances.

Modification (2)

The front may be extended so the edges of the hood overlap at the centre neckline (a). The hem allowance may be converted to a seam allowance for a lined hood (b). The back may be elongated into a long (c) or short (d) point.

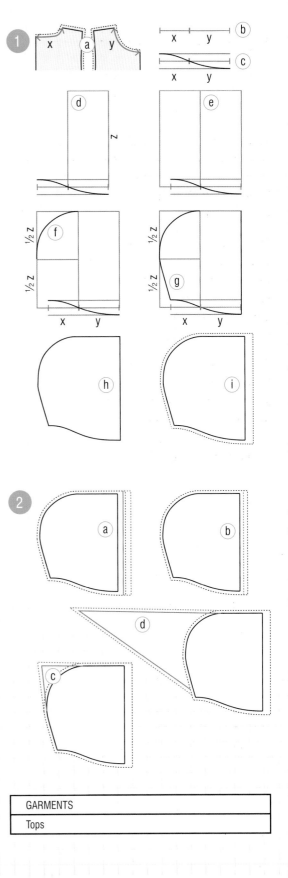

GARMENTS

Tops

Clothing: Carla Hegeman Crim of Scientific Seamstress. Photography: by Mari Hodge of Mari H Photography.

Coats and jackets

No matter the season, overgarments are useful, practical items and there are numerous ways to customise their look. In addition to the collar and hood options listed in this section, you can add patch pockets (see page 52), side pockets (see page 86) or vents (see page 97). Depending on your choice of fabric, you can make anything from a lightweight wrap to a heavy-duty parka. Waterproof fabrics like vinyl and laminated cottons are great for raincoats. Overgarments may be lined or faced (see page 20), or a combination of both, so the item is the appropriate weight and nicely finished.

This block pattern is designed for a loose fit that can be easily worn over clothing. Compared to the basic block, the armholes are dropped significantly. The shoulder seams overhang the shoulder by quite a large margin as well. The sleeve has a wide, roomy cut, and its bottom edge falls slightly below the wrist line, as indicated by the basic/modified block overlay.

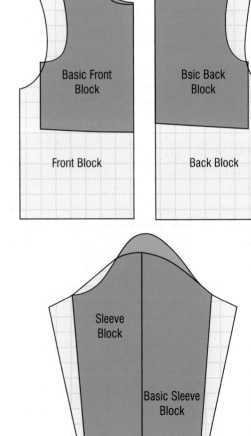

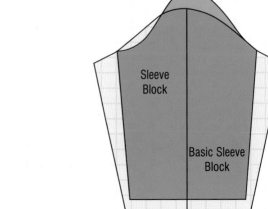

Basic Front Block

Bsic Back Block

Front Block

Back Block

Sleeve Block

Basic Sleeve Block

Clothing and photography: M&Co.

Front placket modification

The block pattern includes cutting/folding lines for a self-facing that is 5cm (2in) wide, a good size for buttoning up and keeping out the chill. The placket can be modified to accommodate different closures and styles.

Zip modification (1)
Move the placket edge in so that it is 1.5cm (⅝in) from the centre front line.

Facing separation (2)
Draw the cutting line 0.6cm (¼in), or other seam allowance width, to the right of the fold line for the front piece (a). Draw the cutting line 0.6cm (¼in), or other seam allowance width, to the left of the fold line for the facing piece (b).

Facing modification (3)
For self-facing, cut the front block at the fold line (a). For a separate facing, add seam allowances as described in (2). Flip the placket over and move the inner edge to the desired position (b), keeping the outer edges the same as the placket on the front piece. For self-facing, re-attach the pieces at the fold line (c).

Placket modification (4)
Cut the front block at the centre front line (a). For best results, make a mirror-image piece to give a sense of size and placement (b). Draw the new placket edge and add the seam allowance to make the front piece (c). Create a facing of the desired shape (d).

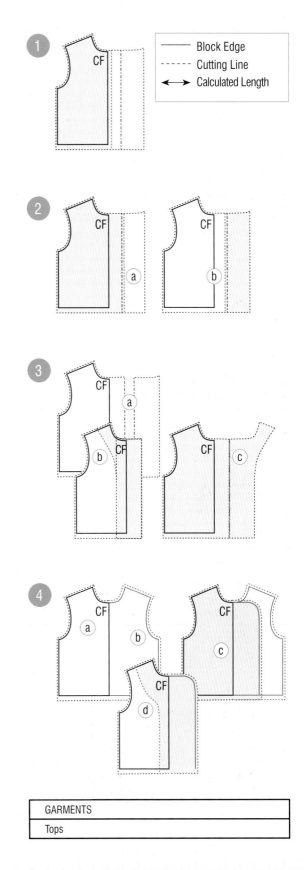

| Block Edge |
| ----- Cutting Line |
| ←→ Calculated Length |

| GARMENTS |
| Tops |

Collars

1. For a standing collar, extend straight up from the neckline edge.

To draft:
a) Measure the back neckline (x) and the front neckline (y). For an overlapping collar, measure the desired distance beyond the centre front line (z).
b) Draw a line the length of x. Make a mark and extend the line by the length of y.
c) Draw a box with the base at xy that is the desired finished collar height.
d) Make a mark 1.2cm (½in) above the lower right corner. Connect this mark to the mark between x and y with a gentle curve.
e) Make a mark 1.2cm (½in) to the left of the top right corner. Connect this mark to the mark made in the previous step.
f) Eliminate the box markings that fall outside the collar. For overlapping collars, extend the front edge with a box the width of z. Smooth the top edge into a curve and trace.
g) Add hem seam allowances.

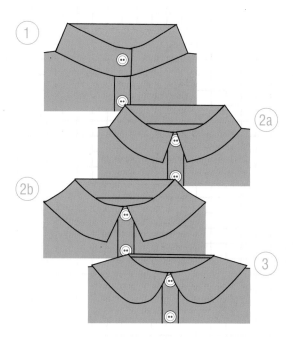

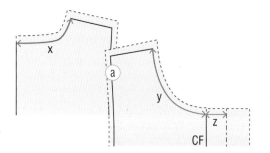

Clothing and photography: M&Co.

2. Convertible: folded collars with a built-in stand.

To draft collars up to 7cm (2¾in) wide (2a):
a) Measure the back neckline (x) and the front neckline (y). For a collar with edges that meet in the front when the garment is closed, measure to the centre front line. To leave a gap, measure to the appropriate point on the neckline.
b) Draw a line that is the length of x. Make a mark and extend the line by the length of y.
c) Draw a box with the base at xy that is the desired finished collar height.
d) Make a mark 1.2cm (½in) above the lower right corner. Connect this mark to the mark between x and y with a gentle curve.
e) Make a mark 2.5cm (1in) to the right of the top right corner. Connect this mark to the corner and the mark made in the previous step.
f) Eliminate the box markings that fall outside the collar.
g) Add seam allowances.

To draft collars wider than 7cm (2¾in) (2b):
Perform steps a–f as described in (2a).
g) Divide the collar into five sections at the base.
h) Slash and spread so the top corners of the sections are 0.3cm (⅛in) apart.
i) Trace and connect the outer edges.
j) Add seam allowances.

3. Flat collars: Extend from the neckline and lay flat against the garment. See page 118 for drafting instructions.

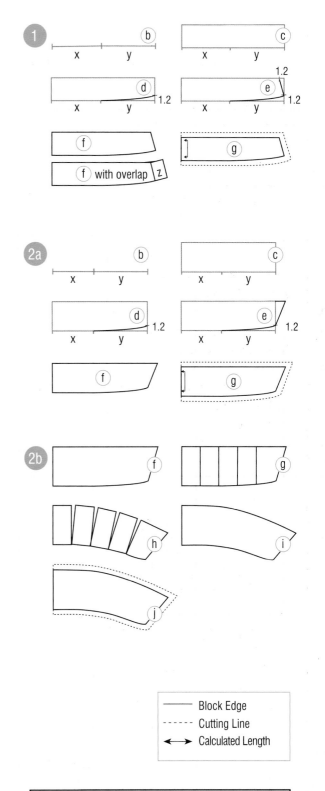

Block Edge
Cutting Line
Calculated Length

GARMENTS
Tops

Hoods

1. Drafting (1)

Two-piece hood draft: Measure and draft, as described on page 59.

Three-piece hood modification: Draft a two-piece hood, as described on page 59. Move the top/back line 5cm (2in) in towards the centre (a). Add the seam allowance to the new side piece (b). Measure the top/back line of the side piece (c). Then draw a rectangle that is this length and 10cm (4in) wide. Add seam and/or hem allowances to complete the centre piece (d).

2. Extending and shaping (2)

Draft the hood as described an 1(a).

Two-piece hood (2a): Draw a box at the front edge that is the width of the desired overlap (b). Draw a smooth curve from the centre top to the bottom right corner (c), or a draw an arc to make a face opening with a bottom tab (d). Add seam/and or hem allowances (not shown).

Three-piece hood (2b): Draw a box at the front edge of the side piece the width of the desired overlap (b). Draw a smooth curve from the top left corner to bottom right corner (c), or a draw an arc to make a face opening with a bottom tab (d). Optional: shape the front edge of the centre front with a slight curve (e). Add seam/and or hem allowances (not shown).

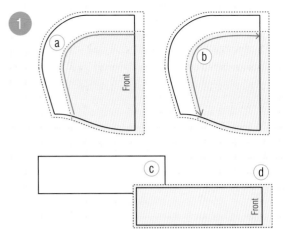

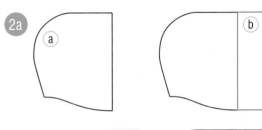

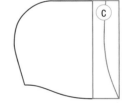
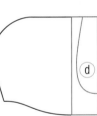

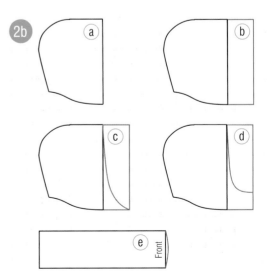

Adding fullness

The blocks can be modified for a fuller base. This adds femininity and allows for movement, particularly in longer garments. Note: After modifying the block pieces, redraw seam, hem and placket allowances.

1. Slash (a) and spread (b) the front and back block pieces to give an A-line shape (c), as described on pages 38–39.

2. Split the front and back blocks with princess seams, as described on page 116 (a). Draw dividing lines at the waistline (b). Slash (c) and spread (d) each bottom, as described on page 39. Trace the flared pieces (e).

3. Draw dividing lines at the waistline or higher (a) and cut the block pieces at the lines (b). Widen the bottom halves to the desired fullness for gathering and attaching like a skirt (c).

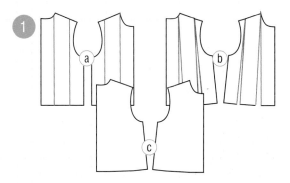

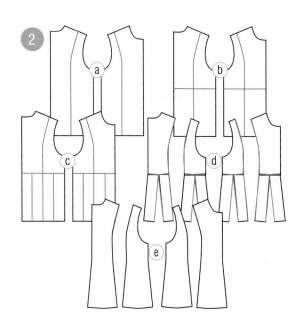

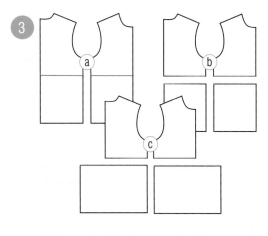

Clothing and photography: Marks & Spencer.

GARMENTS
Tops

Waistcoats

Trendy yet traditional, the waistcoat is a stylish little piece. For formal attire, it can be made from dressy fabrics and worn with a button-up shirt and tie. For a more casual look, use fun cotton prints and pair with a T-shirt. The waistcoat can be simple and straightforward, or jazzed up with design details like collars, mock pockets and back belts.

The waistcoat block provided has sufficient armhole depth to be worn over a shirt. This can be modified to be more loose or fitted, as described on page 55. The bottom edge falls between the waist and hip, and is shaped into a point at the front.

Bottom modification (1)
The waistcoat blocks may be lengthened or shortened, as described on pages 36–37. The point at the bottom edge may be lowered to make a sharper point (a), raised for a less acute point (b), or removed for a flat base (c).

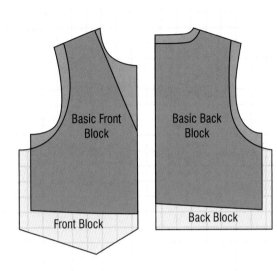

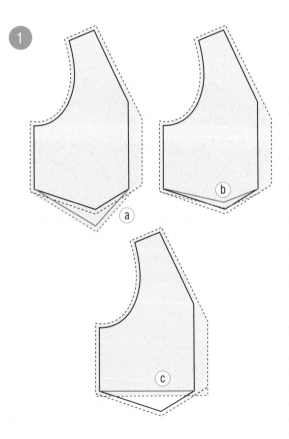

This page: Clothing and photography: Melissa Shelby.
Opposite: Clothing and photography: Debenhams.

Neckline modification (2)

The front block provided (a) has a classic V-shaped neckline that can be lowered (b) or raised (c) as necessary. The neckline may be converted to a curve and lowered (d) or raised (e) to move closer to the natural neckline. The neckline can be rounded off at the centre front to make lapels worn up or folded down (f).

Overlap modification (3)

The front block includes a cutting line that gives a 2cm (¾in) overlap at the centre front (a). For a waistcoat with a zip, position the cutting line 1.5cm (⅝in) from the centre front line (b). For a waistcoat that is open at the centre, move the cutting line the desired distance inwards (c). For a double-breasted look, extend the overlap (d).

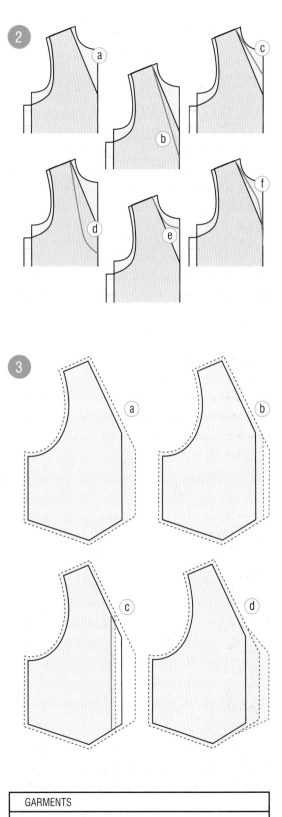

TIP

For best results, place the waistcoat block over the basic block when modifying the neckline. This will give a good sense of shape and position.

GARMENTS
Tops

Adding decorative elements

Collars (1)

Make neckline modifications described on the previous page, if desired. Sketch out the collar on the waistcoat front pattern (a). Repeat for the waistcoat back pattern, making sure the front and back collar pieces match up at the shoulder seams (b). Add the seam allowances (c).

Mock pocket openings (2)

Cut a strip of paper to the desired width, such as 1.2–2.5cm (½–1in), depending on garment size and personal preference. Place over the front waistcoat piece and trim until you have the length and shape you desire. Trace around the edges to mark the placement on the pattern (a). Add seam allowances and a fold placement arrow to the pocket pattern piece (b).

Back ties or belts (3)

Full ties/belts/ribbons are sewn into the side seams and span the entire back. Half ties/belts/ribboms are sewn directly to the outside back, about halfway between the centre back and side edges. Draft ties as described on page 77 (a). Mark the end placement on the back pattern piece (b).

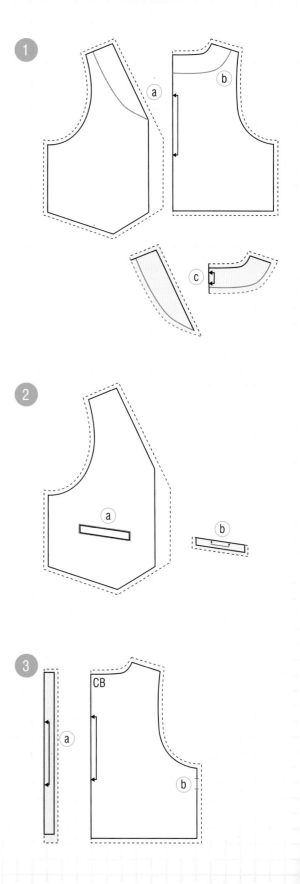

Costume ideas

As simple as they are to make, waistcoats are considered 'dress-up' garments, and are well suited to special occasions and costumes for boys and girls alike. For a quick costume solution, use felt, skip the lining and focus on the embellishments.

Cowboy/Cowgirl
Use denim or a sturdy dark-coloured fabric, and exaggerate the front points. Embellish with some western-themed appliqués or embroidery designs.

Clown
Colourful, mix-and-match prints are your best choice. Substitute a ruffle (see page 118) for the collar.

Handsome prince
Add a collar and faux pockets. Use a rich brocade for the front and fancy satin for the back. Pair with a necktie.

Hippie
Elongate the waistcoat to hip length. Snip or sew on fringing. Add 1970s-themed appliqués like peace signs, doves and rainbows.

Punk rocker
Break out those tartans and embellish with belts, buckles and spikes. Add flair with buttons.

Scarecrow
Use rough fabric like burlap or canvas. Eliminate the lining and allow the edges to fray. Sew on patches to add to the rustic look.

Vampire
Think blood red and midnight black for the base fabrics. Add silky collars and mock pockets for a formal look.

Opposite: Clothing and photography: Angela Bergsma of Vintage Pearl Clothing. **This page top:** Clothing and photography: Tu at Sainsbury's. **This page bottom:** Clothing and photography: Angela Vickers of The House of Lux.

Tunic

Around the globe, the tunic is a cool, stylish favourite. These blocks make for a tunic with a relaxed fit and a slight silhouette. It is a pullover, which means it can be worn and taken off without large openings in the front or back. However, a slit or small cut-out must be added to the front or back to accommodate head size. The neckline opening is finished with a facing. Alternatively, a placket may be added to make a button-up shirt (see page 50). The back is the same width as the front, and has the same armhole shape. The sleeve is cut on the fold, as both sides are the same. The shoulder seams fall slightly below the shoulder level on the arm. The sleeve should fall at wrist level, but can be shortened to cap, short or three-quarter length.

Neckline sizing

The minimum head opening size is 56cm (22in). To determine the correct opening size of the block neckline, measure the front and back neckline and add together. Subtract the result from 28cm (11in), half the minimum opening, to determine how much the opening should be increased.

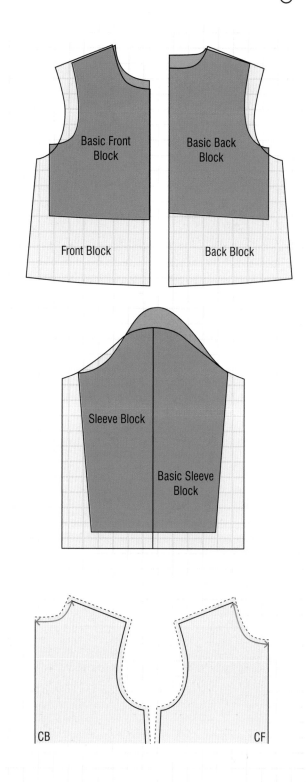

Neckline options

Shape (1)

A slit (a) is the simplest opening to add to the front or back of the tunic. It is cut on the centre line from the neckline to the desired point and stitched to a facing with a very small seam allowance. A drop or keyhole shape (b) is similar but can be slightly higher and still add the same amount of length to the opening. Also, the neckline may be expanded slightly, allowing the bottom of the opening to be raised even higher (c).

Facings (2)

After the neckline is determined, a facing is created. The facing can be placed on the inside of the garment in the traditional fashion, or it can be placed on the outside to add contrast. The neckline and shoulder edges should trace along those of the front or back piece, but the outer edges may vary. For a simple front slit, a V-shaped facing works nicely (a). The size of the back facing is determined by the front facing, as they must match at the shoulder edges (b). For a more intricate keyhole style, the facing can be shaped to echo the neckline (c).

Closures

Ribbon ties and buttons or button loops may be added so the garment can be fastened.

Clothing: Jennifer Paganelli and Carla Hegeman Crim of Sis Boom. Photography: Annie Heng-Tse of Ella Sophie Photography.

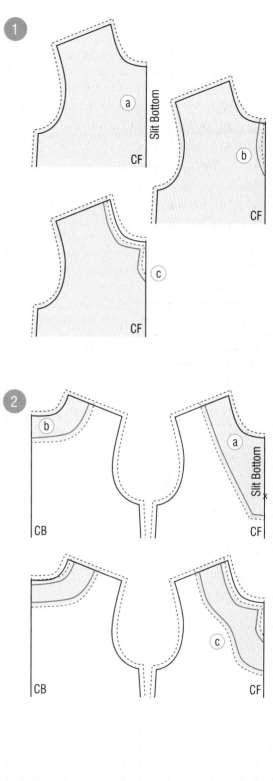

GARMENTS
Tops

Sleeve modifications

The full-length sleeve block (1) is just over wrist length on a child of average height for the given size. Since it is not tapered at the wrist, it has a slight bell shape.

For a ruffled bell sleeve (2), cut the sleeve block near elbow level and add the seam allowance (a). Cut the bottom piece to the width needed to give the desired fullness and add seam allowance (b). Add an arrow to indicate placement on fold (c).

To make a flared bell sleeve (3), mark the centre of the inner sleeve edge with an x (a). Then make a slightly slanted 2.5cm (1in) line to left of the bottom sleeve corner (b). Connect the x to the free end of the slanted line with a slightly curved line (c). Add the seam and hem allowances (d).

Note: because of the flared shape of the sleeve bottom, it is best to finish it with a small, double-folded hem or a facing (see page 20).

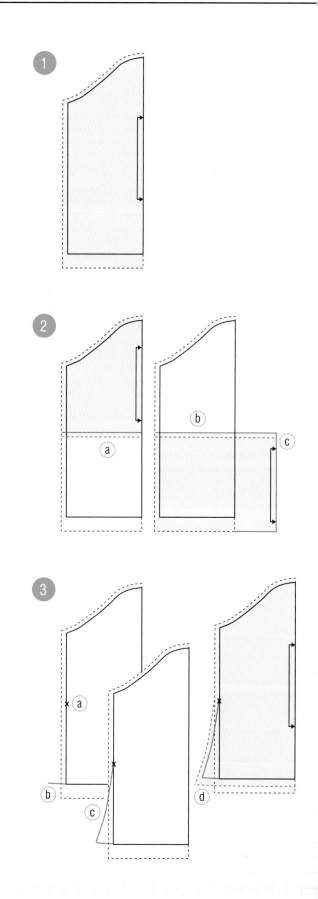

Bottom finishing options

The tunic pattern is drafted to fall around hip length but may be lengthened or shortened, as described on pages 36–37. Although they are not necessary for movement, vents may be placed at the side seams (see page 97 for drafting instructions). Contrasting bands are a nice addition to the bottom edge.

Attached band (1)

Draw a line at the desired position of the band seam on the front piece (a). It should be curved to echo the existing bottom edge. Draw the seam allowance below the line to make the new front piece (b). Draw the seam allowance above the line to create the band piece (c). Trace the line on to the back piece and repeat the process.

Facing (2)

Modify the bottom edge of the front piece to have a seam allowance rather than a hem allowance (a). Draw a facing pattern, as described on page 20 (b). Note: The facing may be shaped to border vent edges.

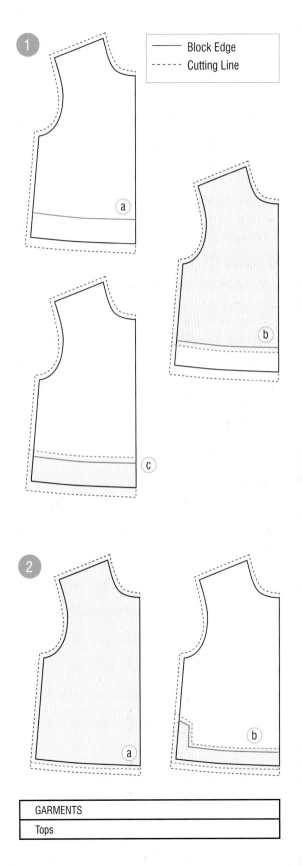

Block Edge
Cutting Line

Opposite: Clothing: Jennifer Paganelli and Carla Hegeman Crim of Sis Boom. Photography: Annie Heng-Tse of Ella Sophie Photography. This page: Clothing and photography by Tu at Sainsbury's.

GARMENTS
Tops

Corsets and halters

Unlike the binding garments of old, contemporary boutique-style corsets are cute and comfortable. They are usually waist length and feature a flat front, ideal for embellishment, and a stretchy back that hugs the body. They can be worn over peasant-style dresses (page 110) to enhance fit and add a whimsical touch. With the addition of ties or straps, corsets also make for cool stand-alone tops. Girls' halters are usually fitted in the chest and looser around the waist and hips. This summertime favourite can be made in a range of lengths and may have built-in or attached straps.

A basic corset pattern is provided where the bottom edge extends a little below the natural waistline. It has an arc shape at the top, which can be modified into different corset and halter shapes. The back block is significantly wider than the basic block so that, when elasticised, it can be pulled on and off easily.

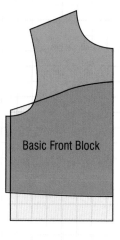

Basic Front Block

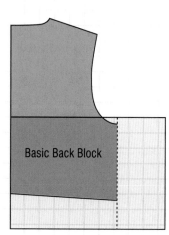

Basic Back Block

Clothing: Andrea Thomas-Lambe of Thomas Parks Gifts.
Photography: Samantha Provenzano of Puddle
Jumpers Photography.

Corset

Fit control (1)

The back is fully elasticised with either shirring (a) or wide elastic contained within channels or casings (b).

Front shaping (2)

The top edge of the provided front block (a) can be reshaped into different styles like sweetheart (b) or pointed (c).

Ties (3)

If the corset is to be worn without a shirt underneath, ties like straps or ribbons should be added to prevent slippage. A single tie can be attached in the centre (a), or two ties can be placed on either side of the neckline (b).

Embellishment options (4)

Corsets are great for adding fun, fancy elements that kids will love. Ruffles at the top (a) and bottom edges (b) add cuteness and coverage. The front can be split into multiple pieces to make a panel for mock or real lacing (c).

To split: Draw a line at the desired position of the seam (d). Redraw with seam allowances to the right (e) and to the left (f) of the line.

TIP

Ribbon tabs and Cluny lace make great 'eyelets' for lacing. Alternatively, ribbon edges can be sewn into the seam in a criss-cross fashion.

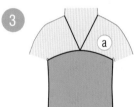

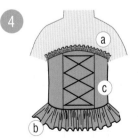

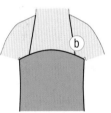

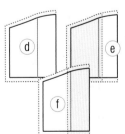

GARMENTS
Tops

Halter

Fit control (1)

The top of the back is elasticised with several rows of shirring (a) or wide elastic contained within a casing (b). For a more fitted style, it can be fully elasticised, as described for the corset (see page 75).

Front shaping (2)

The top edge of the corset block provided can be reshaped into different halter styles. The top edge can easily be raised and straightened for a bib-style neckline (a). The front can be drafted with built-in straps and a square (b) or V-shaped (c) neckline. The bottom edge can be raised for an empire cut so that a skirt piece (see page 113) can be attached (d). The empire length is really suited for crossover styles. The neckline can be extended to intersect with the bottom line (e) or shaped in a smooth curve to meet the side edge (f).

When drafting crossover pieces, it is helpful to place the mirror image of the block at the centre line to gauge the length and positioning of the extension.

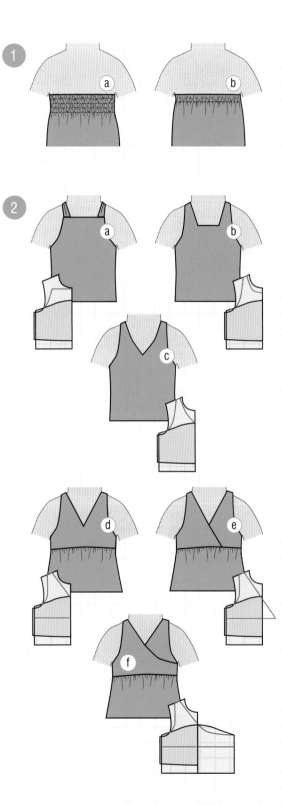

Clothing and photography: Jennifer Baker of Handmade by Jenn.

Straps

Ties (1)

Ties can be made in a range of lengths and widths. Shorter straps (a) can be knotted at the neck, while longer straps may be tied into bows (b). In most cases, 30cm (12in) is long enough for knotting, and 50cm (20in) is sufficient for tying. Wider straps may require more length, depending on the thickness of the fabric.

For lightweight tops, thin straps – less than 2.5cm (1in) wide – provide adequate hold and sit nicely (c). For heavier skirted or embellished tops, the strap should be 2.5–5cm (1–2in) wide to stop drooping and cutting at the neckline (d). Extra wide – 5cm (2in) or more – straps may be used, but they should be gathered or pleated at the attachment point (e). Tie ends can be blunt, pointed or rounded.

Drafting (f): Draw the strap to the finished length and width. Shape the end as desired. Add seam allowances, plus an additional 0.6cm (¼in) at the attachment end.

Back attachment (2)

A loop (a) or tab (b) can be added to the centre back so that ties can be passed through and tied lower on the back.

Built-in straps (3)

Built-in straps are an extension of the pattern on the front.

Drafting: Place the front and back blocks together at the shoulder lines (a). Place the halter front pattern over the front block (b). Then extend the neckline and armhole edges to form a strap that curves around the back neckline (c). Extend to desired length and end shape (d).

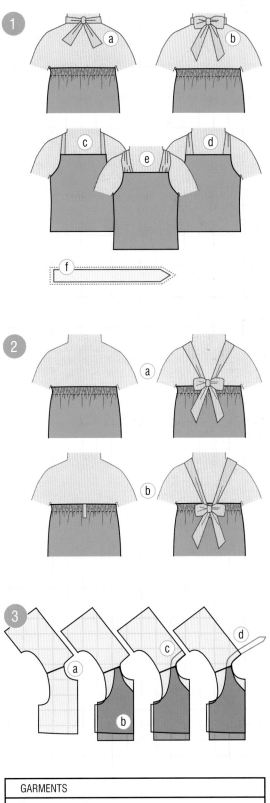

GARMENTS
Tops

Clothing and photography: Bonnie Ferguson of Fishsticks Designs.

Chapter 6
Trousers

From crisp and dressy to soft and casual, trousers are great for active kids. The classic chinos can be made with all the fancy details – a fly, pockets and pleats. They can also be modified to have an elasticised back so the zip may be omitted. Single-seam trousers are easy to sew and wear, and make wonderful pyjamas. Knit leggings and yoga pants are comfortable and practical, and they are also great for sports or just keeping the legs warm. Trousers can be cut in a range of shorter lengths, from capris to short shorts. Add an elasticised casing to make cute little knickers, or bloomers.

Basic Trousers

Trousers, shorts, pantaloons, capris, knickers, leggings – so many types of bottoms are possible from a pattern for basic trousers. A single block pattern is provided for all the trousers in this section. Trousers made with the unmodified pattern are relatively fitted in the waist and hips but more relaxed in the seat and thighs to allow for comfortable movement. The overall fit may be modified, as described on pages 36–37. The top edge is designed to sit at the natural waistline, but it can be raised or lowered for a different look and fit (see page 38). The side seam may be eliminated for an easy-to-make 'single pattern' variation (see page 88).

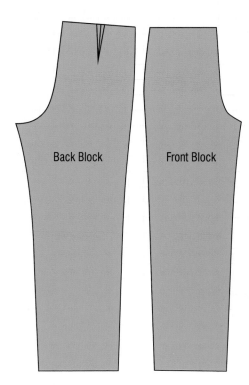

Back Block   Front Block

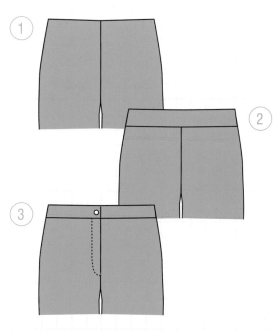

Clothing: Carla Hegeman Crim of Scientific Seamstress.
Photography: Mari Hodge of Mari H Photography.

Front options

The top edge can be finished with a facing (1), or a waistband may be added (2). For both 1 and 2, the back must include an invisible zip opening (see page 82) or an elasticised waistband. If a fly is added to the front (3), the back does not need to be modified. However, an elasticised waistband can be added for extra comfort.

Faced front (1)

To create a facing for the top edge of the block pattern (a): Draw a line at the desired bottom edge of the facing to create the facing piece (b). Then cut away the seam allowance at the centre front line of the facing piece (c). Make a mirror image piece, and align at the centres (d). Smooth out the top and bottom edges (e). Add the top seam allowance and a bottom fold or finishing allowance (f).

Flat front with waistband (2)

Draw a line at the desired seam position on the front block (a). Cut the block at this line. Add on the top seam allowance to create the front trouser pattern (b). To make the waistband: Perform steps (c) through (e) as described in (1). Add the top and bottom seam allowances (f).

Fly front with waistband (3)

Perform steps (a) and (b) as described for (2). Add a fly extension (c) that is 3.2cm (1¼in) wide by the desired length – 15–20cm (6–8in) depending on the size and style. For the waist piece: Move the centre front line the length of the fly extension (d) and add seam allowances (e). Optional: Create a fly facing for one or both sides of the fly (f).

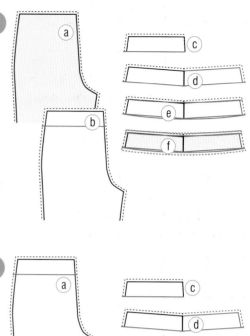

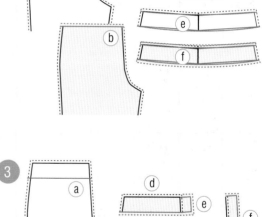

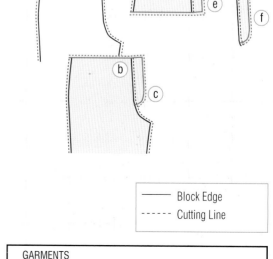

——	Block Edge
- - - -	Cutting Line

GARMENTS
Trousers

Back options

The back can have an invisible zip (1),
a waistband (2), a self-casing for elastic (3)
or an elasticised waistband (4).

Invisible zip (1)

Increase the centre back seam allowance to 1.2cm
(½in) (a). To create a facing for the top edge of
the block pattern: Draw a line at the desired bottom
edge of the facing (b) and cut or trace to make the
facing piece (c). Cut (d) and rejoin (e) at the dart
lines. Smooth out the top and bottom edges (f).
Add the top seam allowance and a bottom fold or
finishing allowance (g). Then add the desired fold
allowance to the centre back edge of the facing (h).

Waistband (2)

Draw a line at the desired seam position on the front
block (a). Cut the block at this line. Add the top seam
allowance to create the back trouser pattern (b). To
make the waistband: Perform steps (c) through (e)
as described in (1). Cut away the centre back seam
allowance (f). Make a mirror image piece, and align
at the centres (g). Smooth out the top and bottom
edges (h). Add the top seam allowance and a bottom
fold or finishing allowance (i).

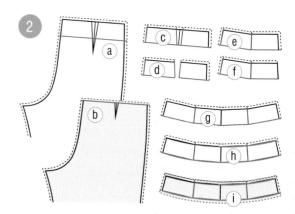

NOTE

If you are adding a front and back waistband, make sure the
pieces are of the same height at the sides.

Elasticized waist with self-casing (3)

Eliminate the dart (a). Draw a line parallel to the waist edge at hip level (b). Cut the block at the line, and tilt the top piece so that there is a 2.5cm (1in) gap at the centre back line (c). Connect the pieces at the centre back block and seam allowance with smooth lines (d). Move the top cutting line up to add the casing (e). Be sure the centre back line kicks out slightly so that the casing will fold neatly.

Elasticized waist with waistband (4)

Perform steps (a) through (d) as described above. Draw a line at the desired seam position on the front block (e). Cut the block at this line. Add the top seam allowance to create the front trouser pattern (f). To make the waistband: Cut away the seam allowance at the centre back line, and add an arrow to indicate that the piece will be cut on the fold at this edge (g). Add the bottom seam allowances (h).

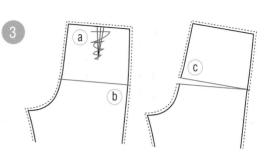

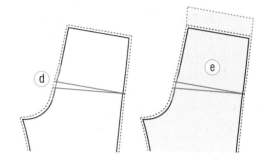

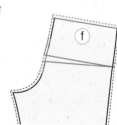

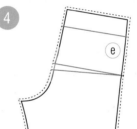

Clothing and photography: Bonnie Ferguson of Fishsticks Designs.

GARMENTS
Trousers

Adding fullness

The front and/or back pieces can be widened to allow for gathers or pleats. Before adding fullness, make the desired fit modifications (see page 80) and draw facings and/or waistbands as described on pages 82–83.

1. To add fullness throughout the leg (1)

Draw a line that extends from the waistband to the bottom edge (a). Cut at the line, and space the pieces twice the desired distance apart* (b). Connect the top and bottom block and seam allowance edges (c). Mark the pleat fold position(s), if applicable.

2. To add fullness without changing the leg opening (2)

Draw a line at knee length that is parallel to the bottom edge (a). Draw a line that extends from the waistband to the knee line at the desired position of the pleat (b). Cut at the line, and then rotate the pieces so that they are the same distance apart* at the top, but still connected to the bottom piece at the outer block edge (c). Connect the top and the bottom block and seam allowance edges (d). Mark the pleat fold position, if applicable (d).

*Note: For pleats, make lines (a) at the desired position of the pleat or pleats. Space the pleats (b) twice the desired pleat depth apart.

This page and opposite: Clothing and photography: M&Co.

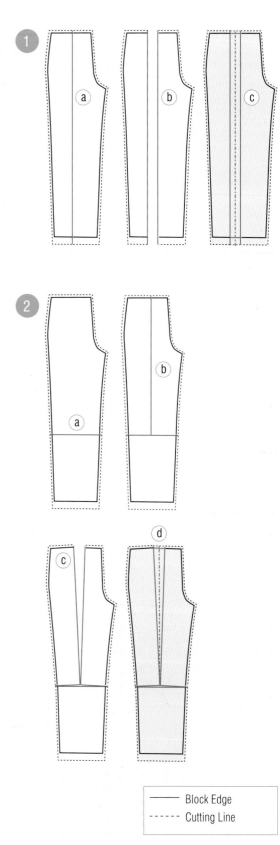

Block Edge
Cutting Line

Leg modification

Flared legs (1)

Draw a line from side seam to inseam at knee level (a). Extend the bottom edge by the desired length on the side seam (b), and repeat on the inseam side (c). Connect the ends of the lines with those of the knee line at the sides (d). Connect the ends at the bottom with a slightly curved line (e). Draw the seam and hem allowances (f). Note: Because of the flared shape, the bottom edge should be finished with a narrow hem or a facing (see page 20).

Tapered legs (2)

Draw a line from side seam to inseam at knee level (a). Mark the bottom edge at the desired position on the side seam of the bottom edge (b), and repeat on the inseam side of the bottom edge (c). Carefully connect the ends of the knee line to the corresponding markings (d). Add the seam allowances (e). Note: To allow for correct folding, drop the seam allowances straight down to the bottom cutting line (f).

Wide legs (3)

Mark the side seam at hip level (a) and the inseam at about 2.5cm (1in) below the crotch point (b). Extend lines straight down to bottom edge level (c) and connect the ends (d). Add the seam and hem allowances (e).

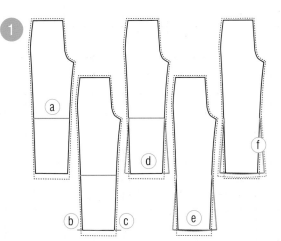

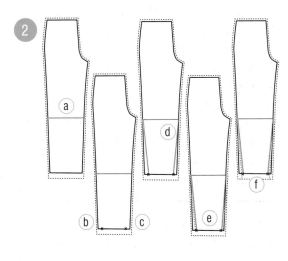

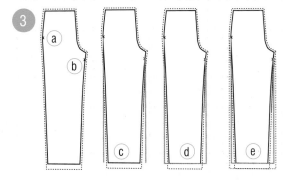

GARMENTS
Trousers

Built-in pockets

Pockets can be attached to the side seam (1), cut away from the front piece and layered over a separate backing (2), or made in the front or back as welt pockets (3).

Drafting

1. Side pockets: Mark an x to indicate the position of the pocket bottom opening (a). Draw a pocket bag that connects to the top edge and is deep and wide enough to accommodate the hand (b). Optional: Draw a facing piece that flanks the opening by about 3.8cm (1½in) (c).

2. Cut-away pockets: Perform steps (a) and (b) as described in (1). Draw a line that connects the top edge to the side edge (c). It may be curved (shown), straight or shaped. Cut the pattern at the line. Add the seam allowance to complete the trouser front pattern (d). Add 3.8cm (1½in) overlap allowance to the cut edge of the remaining piece (e). Place the back bag piece (b, described in 1) over the trouser front pattern. Mark the lines from (c) and (d) to create the front bag piece (f).

3. Welt pockets: Draw a slit at the desired position (a). Draw a bag pattern (b) and welt strip pattern (c). Optional: Make a facing pattern for inside the bag (d).

Patch pockets – See page 52.

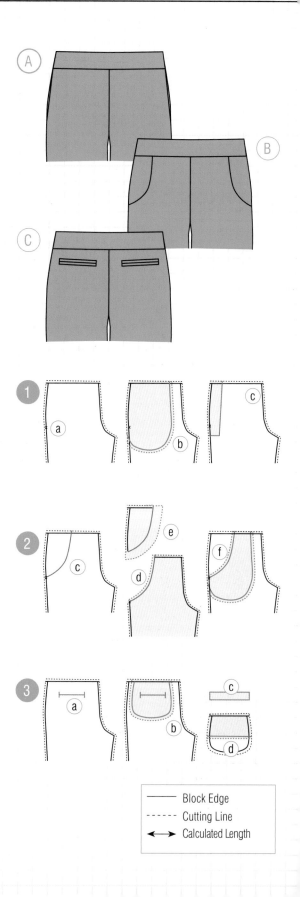

——	Block Edge
- - - - -	Cutting Line
←——→	Calculated Length

Cargo pocket pattern drafting (1)

Draw the pocket to the finished shape and size. Draw lines at the desired pleat positions (a). Cut at the lines, and space the pieces twice the desired pleat depth apart. Connect the top and bottom edges, and make marks to indicate fold lines (b). Add fold allowances at the sides and bottom edges, and add a hem allowance at the top edge (c). Extend the pleat lines to meet the cutting edges. Draw a top flap that is slightly wider than the pocket (d). Add seam allowances at the side and bottom edges, and draw a line to indicate placement on a fold at the top edge (e).

Placement (2)

For patch pockets, place the pocket pattern (without allowances) at the desired position on the pattern and trace (a). For cargo pockets, place the pocket pattern (pleated size, without allowances) at the desired position and trace (b). Make a marking about 1.2cm (½in) above the top edge to mark flap placement, if applicable (c). For larger side pockets (d), place the front and back patterns together at the side block edges and trace as described in (b) and (c).

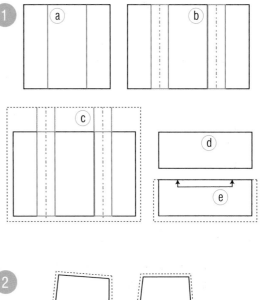

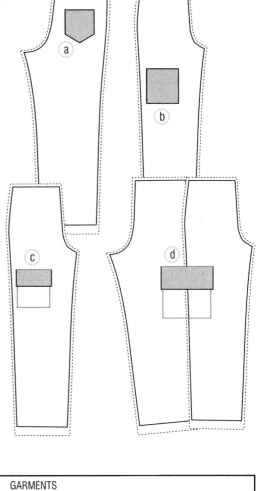

Clothing and photography: Bonnie Ferguson of Fishsticks Designs.

GARMENTS
Trousers

Single-pattern trousers

Also called single-seam trousers, this variation makes for comfortable, easy-sew trousers. This style is great for making cosy pyjamas. Since tapering at the side seam is eliminated, these trousers have a wide-legged look that is perfect for adding contrasting cuffs or ruffles. They are ideal for embellishment with applique or embroidery. Finish with an elasticised casing (see page 83) to make cute knickers.

Drafting (1)

Modify the back trousers block to an elasticised waistband with a self-casing (a). Place the front block next to the back block with the bottom edges in line (b). The blocks should be at least 2.5cm (1in) apart at the hipline. Connect the bottom block and cutting lines (c). Extend the casing allowance to the centre front edge, and drop the cutting line down (d).

Adding contrasting cuffs (2)

Draw a line at the desired seam position (a). Cut the pattern at this line (b). Add seam allowances to both pieces (c). Optional: Increase the hem allowance so it can be folded and stitched just below the attachment seam (d).

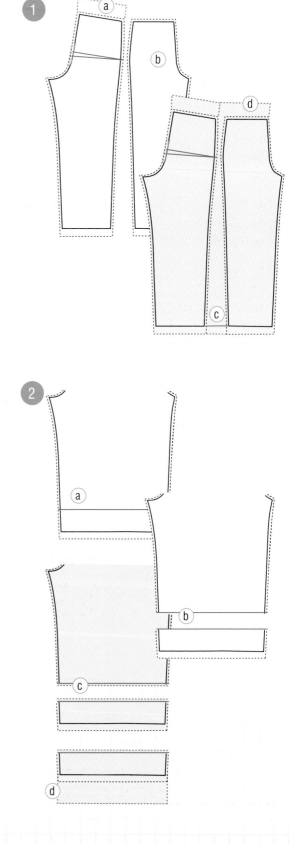

NOTE

Space the blocks further apart at the hipline for even baggier trousers or knickers.

Adding ruffles

Perform (a) and (b), as described on page 88.
Add the seam allowances to the trousers piece (c).
Measure the bottom piece (d) from inseam to side
seam at the top edge (W) and from the top edge to
the bottom block edge (L). This is the finished,
gathered ruffle size. To determine the starting
(ungathered and unfinished) rectangle size,
follow the steps below:

Note: The steps below are illustrated as pattern
pieces; dimensions can be provided in lieu of a
pattern for direct cutting of the fabric.

Single ruffle (1)

Multiply W by the desired fullness factor (usually 2,
see page 102), then add the side seam allowances for
the ruffle strip width. Add the top seam allowance
and bottom hem allowance to L for the correct
ruffle strip length.

Double thickness ruffle (2)

Determine ruffle strip width, as described above.
Add the top seam allowance to L, then multiply by
2 for the ruffle strip length.

For double and triple ruffles, see instructions for
tiering on page 104.

Clothing: Wei Tai-Jiang of One Red Blossom.
Photography: Nena Metcalf.

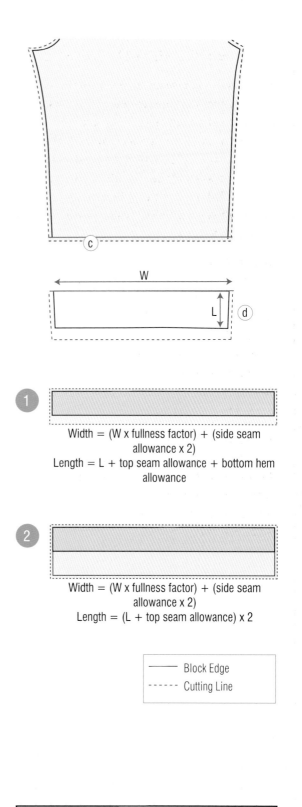

1

Width = (W x fullness factor) + (side seam
allowance x 2)
Length = L + top seam allowance + bottom hem
allowance

2

Width = (W x fullness factor) + (side seam
allowance x 2)
Length = (L + top seam allowance) x 2

——— Block Edge
- - - - - Cutting Line

GARMENTS
Trousers

Knit trousers

Knit trousers are great and comfortable for playtime. Leggings, which are fitted throughout the leg, add an extra layer of warmth and cuteness to any outfit. Yoga pants are fitted through the hips and wide at the legs. They feature a fold-over waistband that eliminates the need for elastic.

Leggings (1)

X = ½ hip measurement

Y = ankle measurement

Place the unmodified front block over the back block with the bottom edges in line. The front and back inseam edges should be X distance apart at the hipline (a). Draw a line the length of Y 5cm (2in) above and centred relative to the bottom edge (b). Connect the ends of Y to the crotch points (c). Add the seam and hem allowances (d). Add a fold line 2cm (¾in) from the top cutting line to indicate the casing allowance (e).

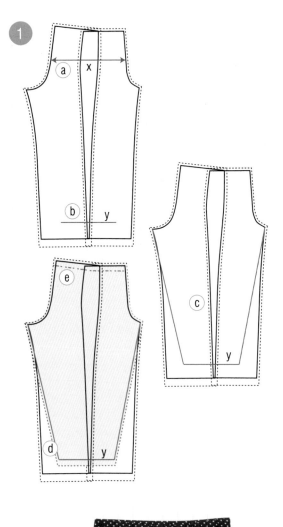

NOTE

Patterns designed for wovens may also be used to make loose-fitting knit trousers. For example, the block patterns provided can be used to make gabardine dress trousers, and the single pattern modification (page 88) is perfect for fleece sweats.

Yoga pants (2)

Modify the back trouser block for an elasticised waist with a waistband, as described on page 83 (a). Place the front block over the back block with the bottom edges in line (b). The blocks should overlap by at approximately 2.5cm (1in) at the hipline. Connect the bottom block and cutting lines (c). Extend the back waist block and cutting lines to the front, and cut away the excess (d).

Waistband: Measure the top edge of the pattern block. Draw a rectangle that is three-quarters this width and also twice the desired finished waistband height, keeping in mind the waistband will be worn folded in half (e). Add seam allowances, a fold line and an arrow to indicate placement on fold (f).

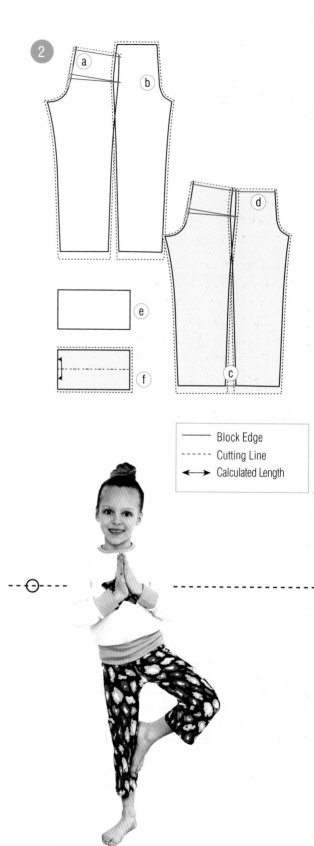

Block Edge
Cutting Line
Calculated Length

NOTE

Knits are highly variable in terms of amount and direction of stretch. Depending on the type of knit you are using and the fit you are after, you may wish to modify the overlap to increase or decrease ease. Length is also dependent on the type of knit. Depending on the amount of stretch, the rise and leg lengths may need to be shortened.

Opposite: Clothing and photography: Tu at Sainsbury's.
This page: Clothing: Amy Hindman of Peek-a-Boo Pattern Shop. Photography: Illusions Images Photography by Angela.

Shorts

For fitted styles, like Bermuda shorts, use the block provided. Make the desired modifications to the front and back waist for a zip and/or elastic. To widen the leg, follow the instructions on page 85. For looser-fitting styles, like board shorts, use the single pattern piece modification (see page 88).

Drafting lengths (1)

For most short lengths, it is simply a matter of drawing a line parallel to the bottom edge at the desired position (a). For shorter shorts that fall at hip level or higher, make sure the bottom edge is no less than 3.8cm (1½in) below the crotch point on the inseam side. For shorts that are only slightly higher than this level, the inseam and side seam can be connected with a straight line (b). For the shortest of shorts, connect with smooth curves, making sure there is ample coverage in the seat area (c).

Lapped shorts (2)

Make desired waistband and fullness modifications, as described on pages 82 and 84. Draw bottom leg opening edges at the desired position (a). Draw overlaps 2.5–5cm (1–2in) beyond the original side seam edge (b). Extend the block and cutting lines at the top edge (c). Note: Edges are usually finished with bias binding, but cute ruffles may also be used.

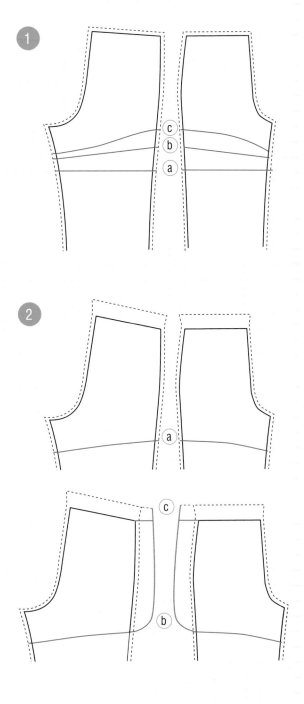

Knickers

These frilly undergarments give a touch of modesty and cuteness to any dress. They also make a great base for sunsuits (see page 133). To draft a pattern for knickers, follow the instructions for single-pattern trousers on page 88. For extra full knickers, set the block pieces 12 to 25cm (5–10in) apart.

For long knickers (pantaloons) (1): Mark the bottom edge parallel to the original bottom edge at the desired position (a). Add the casing or self-ruffle allowance (b).

Self-ruffle allowance = Casing + (desired ruffle length x 2)

For short knickers (panties) (2): Mark 3.8cm (1½in) below crotch level on the side seam (a) and inseam edge (b). Mark the desired finished length position between the blocks (c). Connect with a curved line that levels off near the inseam edges (d). Add the casing allowance (e). Note: Because of the curves, the casing allowance should be kept quite small – 1.2cm (½in) or less. Although self-ruffles are not recommended, the leg edges may be trimmed with a separate ruffle or lace.

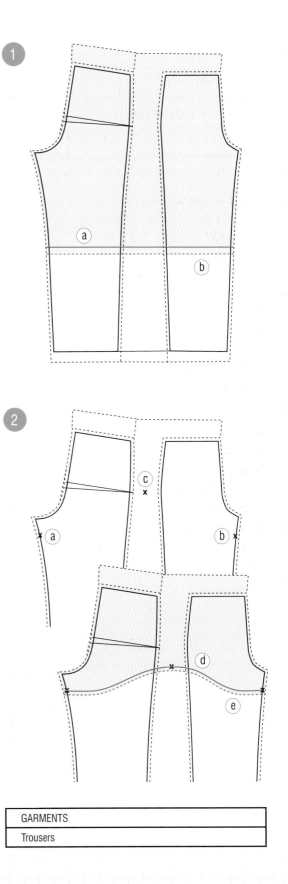

Opposite: Clothing and photography: Tu at Sainsbury's.
This page: Clothing and photography: Janeen Shagman of Dreambirds Children's Boutique.

GARMENTS
Trousers

Clothing and photography: M&Co.

Chapter 7
Skirts

Like trousers, skirts can be straight and serious or full, frilly and fun! For tweens and teens, simple pencil and A-line skirts are popular for school and social occasions. Little girls, on the other hand, love to twirl. Full, fluffy tiered skirts (with or without ruffles) can be designed based on simple calculations. Peplums or overlays may be added for visual interest – perfect for princesses in training. Pleated and circle skirts are classic options for all ages and can be made with a waistband or a yoke.

Basic Skirts

Skirts are easy to design and sew, and are loved by little girls. A sophisticated pencil skirt or classy A-line makes them feel all grown up (but still looking cute). Full, fluffy 'twirl' skirts bring out the inner princess. A single block pattern is provided for fitted skirts. The unmodified pattern makes for a straight pencil skirt with darts, which allows for a snug fit at the waist. It can be easily transformed to make A-line, princess and panelled skirts. Yoke-based skirts may be derived from the block pattern, or a more simple rectangular yoke pattern may be drawn. Elasticised twirl skirts are made from rectangles, which are calculated using simple maths.

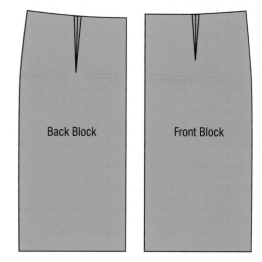

Top finishing options

For dressy, fitted skirts made using the pattern provided, the top edge may be finished using one of the zip, facing and/or waistband combinations described for trousers on pages 82–83.

Lovely skirts can also be made with a flat front (with facing or a waistband) and an elasticised back waist. Mark out or erase the dart (a). Extend the side edge straight up from hip level to waist level (b). Draw a line from the side edge to centre front edge at waist level (c). Connect this line at the centre front edge (d). Add casing and seam allowances (e).

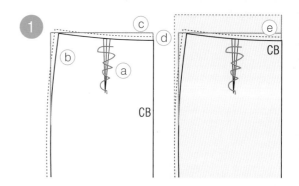

Vents

For fitted skirts that are mid-thigh length or longer, vents (also known as kick pleats) must be added to allow for comfortable movement.

Back vent (1)

The top of the vent should be positioned halfway between knee and hip level for ample movement and coverage. Draw a 4–5cm (1½–2in) wide box from this level to the bottom edge at the centre back (a). Connect the top right-hand corner to the opposite edge with a 45-degree angle (b). Draw the side and bottom edges (c). Remove the box and add fold and hem allowances (d).

Side vents (2)

Since there are two of them, side vents are shorter and narrower than a single back vent. Draft as described above, but make the starting box half the length and width. Position the box on the side edge rather than the centre edge, and draft the extension on both the front and back pieces.

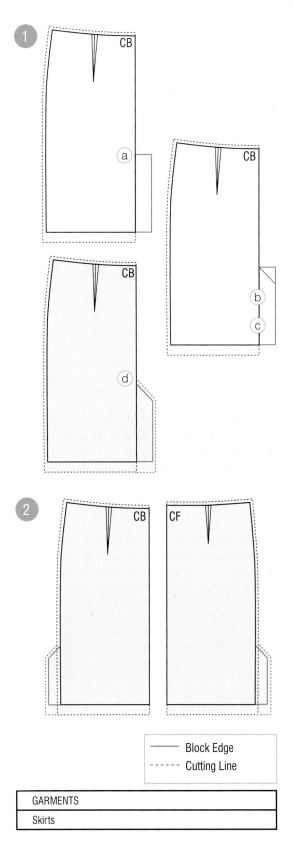

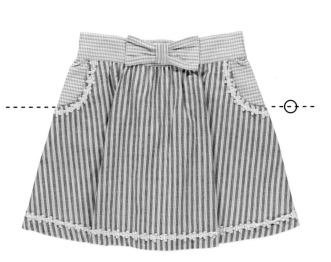

——	Block Edge
- - - -	Cutting Line

GARMENTS
Skirts

Clothing and photography: George at ASDA.

Adding flare

The basic skirt block is easily converted to an A-line shape. For a slightly flared skirt – 2.5–5cm (1–2in) wider at the base on the pattern and 10–20cm (4–8in) on the finished skirt – the side edge is repositioned at an angle. For more flare, slash and spread is used (see pages 38–39).

Slight flare (1)

Draw a slightly angled line that is the desired extension length at the bottom side edge of the back block (a). Connect the end of the line to the side edge at hip level (b). Draw seam and hem allowances (c). Repeat on the front block piece (d).

Full flare (2)

Draw a line from waist to bottom edge at the position of the dart centre on the back block (a). Draw a second line that is halfway between this line and the side seam at waist level (b). Draw an additional line halfway between the first line and the centre front (c). Slash and spread to the desired fullness at the base (d), making sure the pieces overlap at the position of the dart so that it can be eliminated (e). Draw seam and hem allowances (f). Repeat the process on the front block (g).

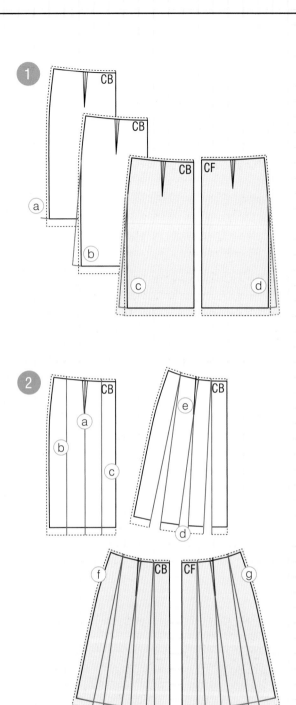

NOTE

For even fuller skirts, use the circle skirt draft (page 106).

Princess seams and panelled skirts

Princess seams (1) eliminate the need for a dart and add design detail to the skirt. They may be added to the front and/or back blocks.

To draft: Draw cut lines on both sides of the dart (a). Extend a line from the bottom of the dart to the bottom edge of the block (b). Cut at the lines (c). Add seam allowances (d).

Panelled skirts (2), also known as gored skirts, are fitted at the top and flared at the bottom. They can be made from a single fabric, or mix and match fabrics and prints for a free-spirited look.

To draft: Follow steps (a) to (d), as described above, and add a seam allowance at the centre edge (e). For each block half, draw a line at the desired flare start point, generally halfway between hip and knee level (f). Draw a line that extends from the centre of the first line to the bottom edge (g). Slash and spread as described on pages 38–39 (h). Connect the bottom edges with smooth curves (i). Add the hem allowance to each piece, keeping in mind that it should be kept small to accommodate the curves (j).

Clothing and photography: Jen Hagedorn of Tie Dye Diva Patterns.

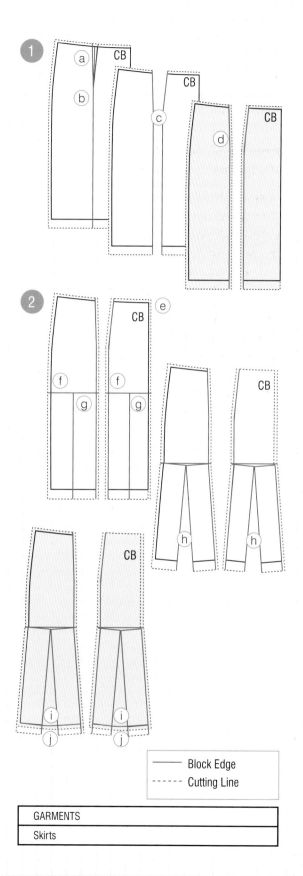

——	Block Edge
- - - -	Cutting Line

GARMENTS
Skirts

Yoke-based skirts

Yoke-based skirts have a relatively trim fit through the waist, hips and an attached bottom piece (see pages 102–107 for options). This allows for a full skirt without bulk at the top.

1. Fitted yokes can be drafted using the provided patterns (see pages 80–83 for top finishing options). For the front and back blocks, draw cutting lines at the desired position (generally hip level), echoing the shape of the waist edge (a). Add the seam allowance (b).

2. Fully elasticised yokes are simple rectangles.

H = desired finished length (generally the waist to hip measurement)
W = (hip measurement + desired ease*) ÷ 2

*For a semi-fitted yoke, 7.5cm (3in) ease is sufficient, but more can be added for comfort, growth and design (see page 22). For fuller 'twirl' skirt yokes, see page 103.

To draft: Draw a rectangle that is H x W (a). For a single-piece yoke with a centre back seam, add the top casing allowance, bottom seam allowance, one side seam allowance and an arrow to indicate placement of the pattern edge on a fold (b). For a two-piece yoke with side seams, add the top casing allowance and side and bottom seam allowances (c).

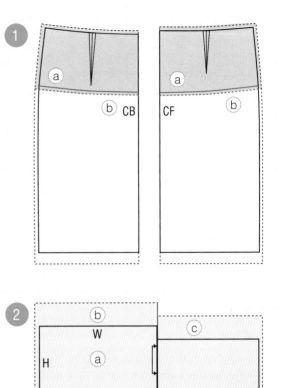

NOTE
Yokes can be shorter, longer or shaped. Make sure to modify the bottom piece accordingly.

Clothing and photography: Monsoon/Accessorize.

Waistbands

1. Shaped waistband – Sits lower on the waist and works well for circle skirts. To draft, draw lines at the desired waistband bottom-edge position on the front and back blocks. Extend the lines up the side edges, and label the centre front and centre back edges (a). Cut the blocks at the lines, and cut away the side seam allowances (b). Mark the dart lines (c) and cut (d). Rejoin the pieces at the dart edges (e). Join the front and back waistband pieces at the side seams (f). Draw a smooth curve at the top and bottom edges (g). Draw the top and bottom seam allowance and add an overlap extension at the centre back (h).

2. Folded strip waistband – Simple to draft, but must be worn fairly snug to prevent slippage.

H = desired finished depth x 2
W = (waist measurement + ½ in) ÷ 2

To draft: Draw a rectangle that is H x W. Draw a line to indicate the fold position (a). Add the top and bottom seam allowances, an overlap extension on one end, plus an arrow to indicate placement of the pattern edge on a fold (b).

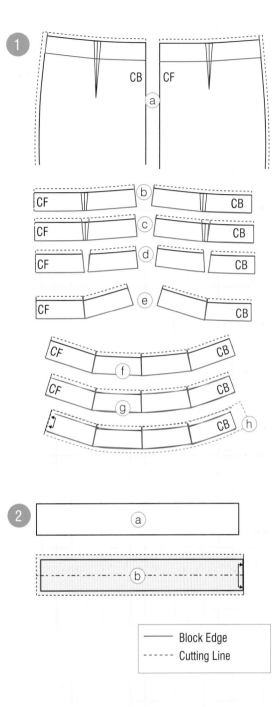

——— Block Edge
- - - - - Cutting Line

NOTE
Zip or placket allowances must be added to skirt pieces that attach to non-elasticised waistbands (see page 121).

GARMENTS

Skirts

Gathers, tiers and ruffles

Fullness factor

For gathered skirts and ruffles, fullness factor (FF) is calculated by dividing the ungathered fabric width by the gathered fabric width. For example, a 100cm (40in) length of fabric gathered to 50cm (20in) has a fullness factor of 2 (also referred to as 2x).

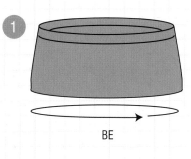

BE

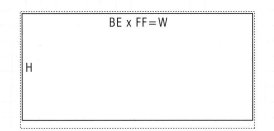

BE x FF = W

H

Factor	Gathering
1.25x	Very light
1.5x–2x	Moderate, good for ruffles and tiers
2x–2.5x	Full, typical for skirts attached to yokes and bodices
2.5x +	Very full, suitable for light fabrics only

Gathered skirts (1)

To calculate skirt or ruffle piece width (W), measure the bottom edge (BE) of the skirt or dress piece to which it will attach, then multiply by fullness factor (FF). Add side seam and/or fold allowances.

Skirt piece height (H) depends on the desired finished length and the length of the attachment pieces. The vertical measurement chart (page 17) is useful for determining how long to make skirt pieces. Add seam and/or hem allowances.

NOTE

Many children's patterns use the full 115cm (45in) width of fabric (WOF) for the skirt, regardless of size. 1 WOF gives a moderately gathered skirt, while 2 WOF gives a very full gathering. For 150cm- (60in-) wide fabrics, 1 WOF gives full gathering.

This page: Clothing and photography: Eucalyptus Clothing.
Opposite: Clothing and photography: Lisa Gay of Aivilo Charlotte Designs.

Tiered skirts

Skirts made from multiple tiers (1) have more fullness than a simple gathered skirt. Use long, lightly gathered tiers for an elegant maxi. For a perky twirl skirt, use short, moderately gathered tiers. The tiers can be made from solid strips or pieced from multiple fabrics for a patchwork look.

Tier width:

Top tier – If the skirt will be attached to a waistband, fitted yoke or bodice, calculate W, as described on page 102. If you are making an elasticised yoke, it will be your top tier. For a full 'twirl' skirt, multiply the waist measurement (see page 14) by the desired fullness factor (usually 1.5x) to determine your yoke width.

Subsequent tiers – Multiply the width of the previous tier by the desired fullness factor.

Tier height:

Determine the desired total finished length of the tiered portion. For equal tiers, divide this length by the number of tiers. Each tier will be this finished length. Add casing, seam and hem allowances to the appropriate pieces to get the tier piece height.

NOTE

Ruffles, tiers and gathered skirt pieces are usually provided as dimensions rather than pattern pieces. It is helpful, however, to draw out scale models during the drafting process to help visualise the pieces.

GARMENTS
Skirts

Ruffled tiers

For ruffled tiered skirts, the tier pieces play a supportive role, as they back and attach ruffles. The tier pieces can be expanded, as described on page 103 (1), or can have the same width throughout for 'rhumba' ruffles (2).

Tier calculation:

Subtract 1 from the number of ruffles to get the number of tiers required.

Determine the desired finished length of the ruffle assembly (top of the top ruffle to bottom finished edge of the bottom ruffle). Divide this by the desired number of ruffles. This will give you the finished tier height. Add seam allowances to get the ruffle piece height. Calculate tier piece width, as described on page 103. For rhumba ruffles, it will be the same as the unfinished bottom edge of the attaching piece (yoke, bodice or trouser leg).

Ruffle calculation:

To calculate finished ruffle height, add the desired overlap (the amount a ruffle hangs over the top of the ruffle or tier below) to the finished tier height. For the bottom ruffle, no overlap should be added. Add seam and hem allowances for ruffle piece height. Calculate ruffle width relative to the bottom edge of the attaching piece. For the top ruffle, this will be the yoke, bodice or trouser leg. For subsequent ruffles, it will be the tier above.

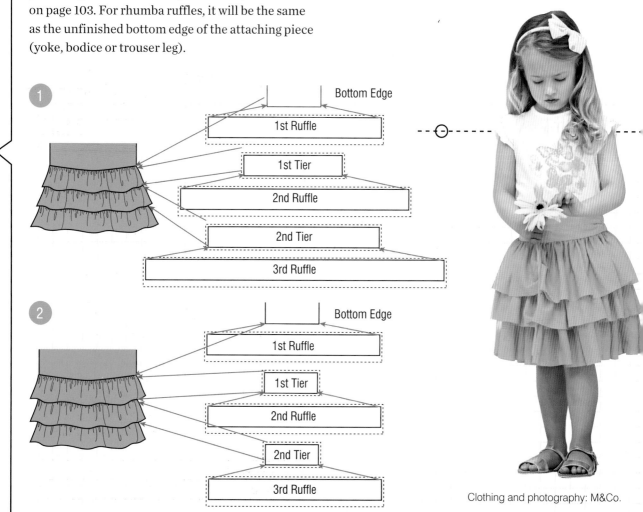

Clothing and photography: M&Co.

Peek-a-boo overlays and peplums

Peek-a-boo overlays and peplums are fun, princess-like elements that are layered atop an underskirt. Peek-a-boo skirts are generally just a little shorter than the underskirt, while peplums are usually short and puffy. Pick-ups (gathers or drawstrings) may be added to the bottom edge.

Peek-a-boo overlay (1)

Draw a rectangle that is the desired width (can be the same as the underskirt or a bit fuller) and height (a). Shape the bottom corners (b). Add seam or thin hem allowances (c).

Bubble peplum (2)

Draw a rectangle that is the desired width (can be the same as the underskirt or a bit fuller) and twice the desired finished height (a). Add seam allowances and the folding line (b). Mark the positions of pick-ups (c).

Pointed peplum (3)

Draw a circle (a) that is the size of the waist opening (see page 106). Draw a square that is the desired size centred at the circle (b). Add seam allowances (c).

Split peplum (4)

Draw a rectangle that is the desired width (can be half the underskirt width or a bit fuller) and twice the desired finished height (a). Shape at all corners (b). Add seam allowances and the folding line (c).

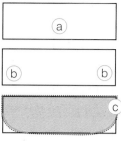

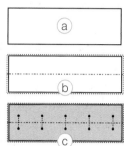

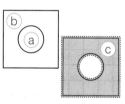

——————	Block Edge
- - - - - -	Cutting Line
— — —	Fold Line
•- - - -•	Gathering Line

GARMENTS
Skirts

Circle skirts and flounces

Simple full and half circles offer fullness without gathering. Flounces are ruffle-like trims made from closely spaced circles. For both circle skirts and flounces, the inner circle is calculated based on the bottom edge measurement (BE) of the attachment piece, as described on page 102. The size of the outer circle depends on the desired length of the skirt or flounce. Note: For skirts attached to waistbands or fitted bodices, a placket or zip extension must be added (see page 121).

Full circle (1)

Divide BE by 3.14 to get the inner circle diameter (ID) (a). Draw a circle with this diameter (b). Determine the desired finished length (L) (c). Multiple L by 2, and add ID to get the outer circle diameter (OD) (d). Draw a circle with diameter centred relative to the first circle (e). Add seam allowances (e).

Half circle (2)

Draft as described for full circle, but divide BE by 1.57 and draw half circles. The resulting pattern can be represented as a half piece that is cut on a fold.

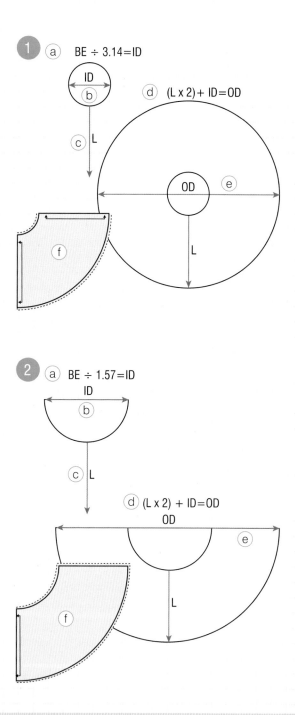

NOTE

To save space and make for easier cutting, 0.6cm (¼in) of the circle can be provided to cut on double folds.

Clothing and photography: Missguided.co.uk.

Pleated skirts

Pleats add fullness and classic design detail to skirts. Deep pleats in heavy fabrics make for preppy kilts. For lighter fabrics, pleats can be used in place of gathers. Knife pleats (1) point in the same direction, while box pleats (2) alternate in opposite directions.

The top pleated edge of the skirt should be the same length as the bottom edge measurement (BE) of the attachment piece, as described on page 102.

Pleat spacing (PS) is the distance from one pleat edge to the nearest fold on the next pleat. Pleat depth (PD) is the width of the fold behind the pleat. PD may be less than or equal to PS.

To calculate: Determine the desired PS (DPS). Divide BE by DPS and round down to the nearest whole number to get the number of pleats (PN). Divide the remainder (number that is behind the decimal point) by PN, and add this number to DPS to get adjusted PS. Determine PD. Multiply PD x PN, then multiply by 2. Add this number to BE to get the starting skirt piece width (W).

To draw: Draw a box that is W by the desired H (a). Make marks to indicate pleating positions (b). Add seam and hem allowances (c). Note: For skirts attached to waistbands or fitted bodices, a placket or zip extension must be added (see page 121).

——————	Block Edge
- - - - - -	Cutting Line
– – – – –	Fold Line

Clothing and photography: Stacey Mann of Hailey Bugs Closet.

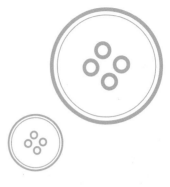

Chapter 8
Dresses

There is nothing like a beautiful dress to make a girl feel special. Many dress styles can be derived from the tops discussed in Chapter 5. Blouses/shirts can be extended into trim-fitting or flared styles. Alternatively, they can be shortened, with a separate skirt attached. Other classic dress styles described include the A-line, bodice dress and jumper dress. All these designs are suited to customisation with appliqué and embellishments to make truly one-of-a-kind creations.

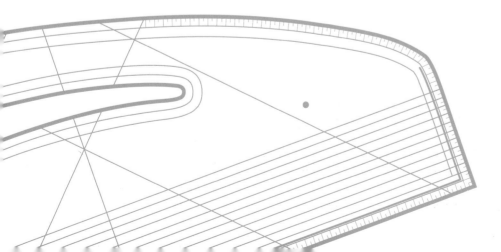

Basic Dresses

All the top options described in Chapter 5 can be modified to become dresses. For a casual look, simply elongate the basic peasant, tunic or T-shirt. To go more over-the-top and fancy, add a full, ruffled skirt to a fitted halter or corset. Ruffled corset dresses over peasant dresses make for regal princess-wear.

Extending basic shirt patterns

Girls' shirt patterns can be converted into dresses by extending and adding fullness, or by shortening and adding a skirt. Waist and hip positions are marked on the patterns. Use the vertical measurement chart (see page 17) to determine your desired finished length.

Peasant dresses

Just like their top length counterparts, peasant dresses are comfortable and easy to make. They can be dressy or casual, depending on the fabric and embellishments.

1. Extension – Lengthen the peasant block by moving the bottom cutting line down (a). Add fullness using slash and spread, as described on pages 38–39 (b). Add hem and seam allowances (c).

2. Skirt addition – Shorten bodice by moving the bottom cutting line up (a). Position it at waist level for a natural waist bodice or closer to the armholes for an empire waist bodice. Add seam allowances (b). Draft gathered skirt piece(s), as described in Chapter 7 (c).

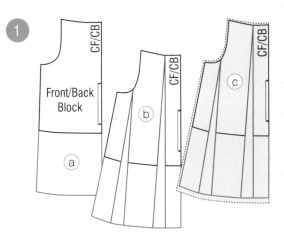

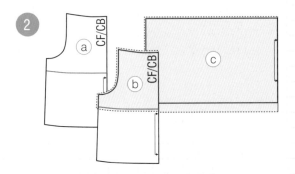

Tunic dresses and shirtdresses

1. Tunic dresses are summery and make for great swimsuit cover-ups. The provided tunic top front and back blocks are easy to extend into a dress of the desired length, as described for peasant dresses. It has ample flare, so additional fullness is not needed. Vents and/or facings may be added as described on pages 73 and 97.

2. Shirtdresses put a feminine spin on a tailored classic. They can be created by simple extension (with or without flare), or they can be made into a bodice with a shirt piece. The shirt front and back blocks provided can be modified to make a shirtdress, as described for peasant dresses. An elongated version (a) can be made by dropping the bottom edge, which can be straight or shaped, as described on page 112. For a skirted bodice version (b), a placket can be added to the skirt so that the dress buttons all the way from top to bottom.

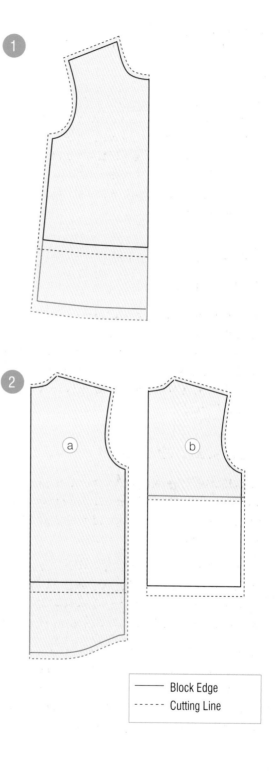

	Block Edge
- - - - -	Cutting Line

Opposite: Clothing and photography: Tiffany Vela and Shannon Donoghue of Create Kids Couture. **This page:** Clothing and photography: Debenhams.

GARMENTS
Dresses

Knit T-shirt dresses

Knit T-shirt dress patterns are very popular for upcycling T-shirts. Since knits are so versatile, there are numerous ways to create a dress from a simple T-shirt pattern.

Extension (1)

a) Simple extension – Move the bottom line down by the desired length to make a straight dress.

b) Extension with fullness throughout – Elongate, then slash and spread the full length of the block pieces, as described on pages 38–39.

c) Extension with fullness below the waist – Elongate, then draw a horizontal line at the desired fullness starting point. Slash and spread below this line.

Skirt addition (2)

The T-shirt block can be shortened to empire length or natural waist length, or it can be left as is for a dropped waist length. Add the seam allowance for skirt attachment.

a) Gathered skirt addition – Draft a gathered skirt piece, as described on page 102. Note: Knit or woven fabrics may be used for the skirt piece. Wovens can be gathered to a higher fullness factor without weighing down the top of the dress.

b) Flouncy skirt addition – Draft a circle skirt, as described on page 106.

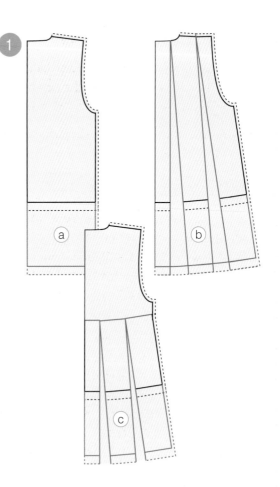

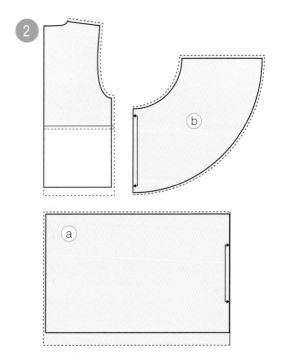

Halter and corset dresses

The very simple halter and corset tops can be converted into beautiful dresses that can be worn alone or layered with other tops and dresses.

Draft a bodice with the desired strap and fit options as described on pages 76–77.

Extension (1)

A slightly flared, trim-fitting halter dress can be made by extension. Extend the front and back patterns by the desired length (a). Draw a horizontal line below the base of the armholes on the front piece (b). Slash and spread below this line (c). Since the back piece has added fullness, no further modification is needed.

Skirt addition (2)

For fuller dresses, add a gathered skirt to a halter or corset bodice. Draft the bodice the desired length, making sure to leave ample length for the skirt attachment in the back (a). Draft skirt pieces, keeping in mind that the shirred/elasticised back bodice is wider than the front bodice. For best results, make the skirt out of two identical pieces – one for the back and one for the front (b). The back will be less gathered than the front when attached, but the skirt will be balanced.

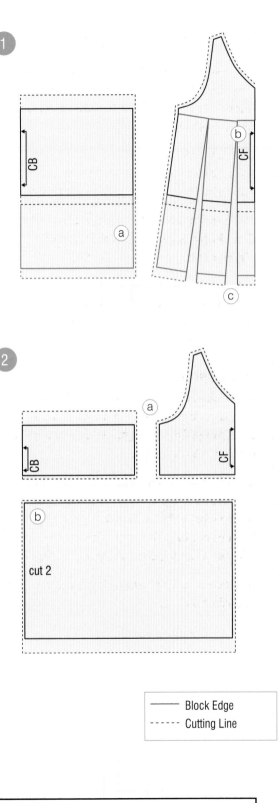

Clothing and photography: Dana White of Silly jillybeans.

	Block Edge
	Cutting Line

GARMENTS
Dresses

A-line

The A-line is a classic modification of the basic bodice dress. It is semi-fitted through the chest, but increases in fullness with length. The A-line pattern provided is approximately knee-length, but can be lengthened or shortened, as described on pages 36–37. This mod style is a great canvas for appliqué and embroidery work. It is also well suited to colour blocking, as described on page 51. Since it is so similar in fit to the basic bodice pattern, the puffed sleeves provided can be added. All the collar options described on page 118 can be applied to the A-line dress as well.

Facings and linings

1. Facings – Since the neckline and sleeve openings are close together, it is easiest to make dual-duty facings. Draw the facing patterns to include the neckline edges and the armhole edges. Draw the outer edges to echo the inner edges, making sure there will be ample material for the facings to lay and launder properly.

2. Linings – The A-line pattern can be used to cut a full lining. Depending on the fabric choices and the finishing, the A-line can be reversible.

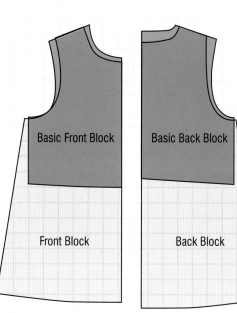

Basic Front Block   Basic Back Block

Front Block   Back Block

Clothing and photography: George at ASDA.

Shoulder opening options

The block pattern provided requires an opening/
fastener at the neckline (see page 120) or some
kind of modification to include a shoulder opening.

1. Shoulder fasteners – This option allows for
easy on, easy off with buttons or snaps (see page
20). The tabs can be rounded, as shown, or squared
off for a different look. To draft: Mark the desired
fastener position, then draw the front tab on the
front bodice block piece (a). Align the front and
back pieces at the shoulder edges, then extend the
back bodice so that the back tab overlaps the front
tab (b). Separate the front and back pieces (c).
Draw seam allowances (d).

2. Back crossover – This modification is fastener-
free and adds cute detail to the back. Since it is
open at the back, it can be worn with pantaloons
or knickers. To draft: Align the front and back block
pieces at the shoulder edges. Include the mirror
image of the back piece. Connect the outer
shoulder/armhole corner with the bottom corner
of the mirror image back piece (a). Connect the
inner shoulder/neckline corner with the armhole/
side seam corner of the mirror image back piece
(b). Add seam allowances to the crossover back
piece (c).

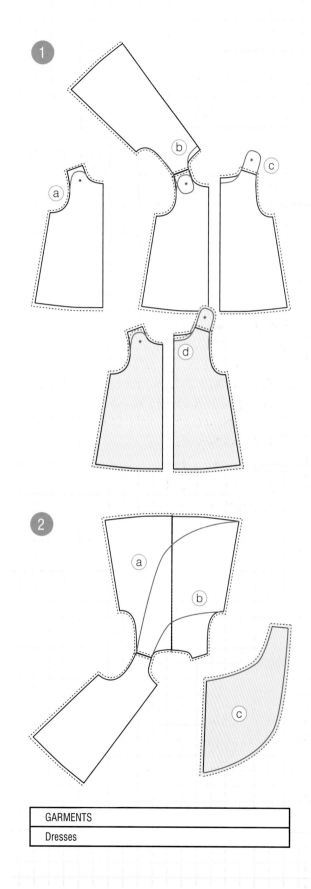

GARMENTS
Dresses

Basic bodice dress

The basic bodice dress is well suited to customisation with unlimited neckline, waistline, collar, sleeve and skirt variations. This classic style is known as the basic bodice dress because the overall cut closely follows the basic bodice block. The block pattern provided makes for a semi-fitted bodice that requires a front or back closure.

Arm openings

The armholes are cut to give a good fit with or without sleeves. The bodice may be finished with facings or a lining (see page 20). Short, puffed sleeves are included, but can be modified to different lengths and/or fullnesses.

Darts

The bodice patterns include small darts that may or may not be sewn, depending on the desired look. Darted bodices (1) will have a more tapered fit that cinches in at the waist, while leaving out the darts (2) gives a roomier waistline.

Princess seams

The darts may be converted to shoulder (3) or armhole (4) princess seams.

Draw cut lines on both sides of the dart (a). Extend a line from the top of the dart to the appropriate edge of the block, curving as needed (b). Cut at the lines (c). Add seam allowances (d).

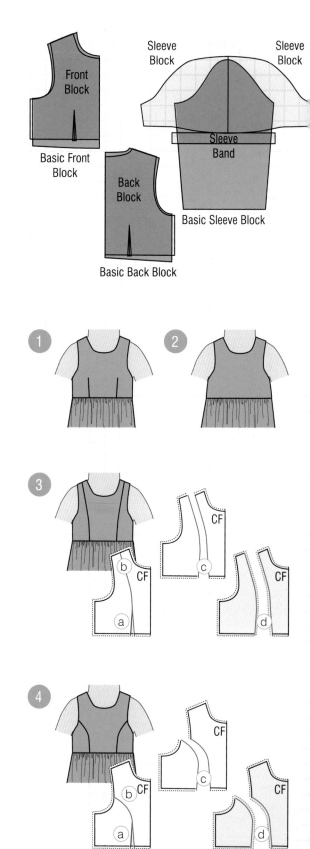

Clothing and photography: Littlewoods.

Neckline modification

Boatneck (1)

Unchanged at the centre front but positioned further away from the natural neckline at the shoulder. It is a good idea to leave at least a centimetre or two for the shoulder seam.

Scoop neckline (2)

Lowered at the centre front and comes up to the shoulder in a gentle curve. Depending on the shape of the scoop, the neckline may need to fall on the shoulder further away from the neckline.

Square neckline (3)

Similar to the scoop neckline in positioning options, but the shape is formed by straight lines rather than a curve.

The 'V' neckline (4)

Comes to a point in the centre front and extends diagonally towards the existing neckline. As with the scoop neck, the shape and shoulder position can vary.

The princess neckline (5)

Similar to the 'V' neckline, except it peaks near the centre, levels off, then shoots back up to the existing neckline.

Regardless of neckline style, if the position of the neckline is modified at the shoulder, align the bodice blocks at the shoulder seam and extend the neckline around the back piece (6).

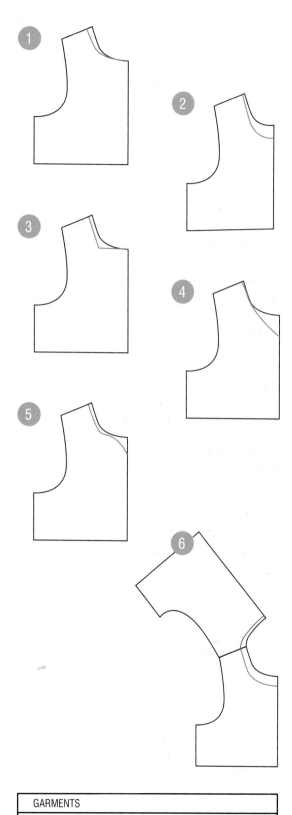

GARMENTS
Dresses

Collars

Flat collars give classic appeal to the neckline. The most popular example seen in children's wear is the Peter Pan collar (1). This two-piece design is rounded in the front and back. Typically, the collar pieces butt up against one another in the finished garment. Depending on the fastener type and/or personal preference, space may be left between the collar pieces.

To draft: Make any neckline modifications needed, as described on page 117. Place the bodice pieces together at the shoulder block edges. Rotate so the pieces overlap by 1.2cm (½in) at the top armhole edges (a). Then draw the collar the desired size and shape, keeping the inner edge the same as the neckline (b). Add seam allowances (c).

Other flat collar variations include:

2. Pointed flat collar.

3. Rounded bib collar (cut on fold to encircle entire front neckline and meet in back).

4. Sailor collar (attached at the back neckline but finished and unattached in the front – generally includes a tie or a bow at the front meeting point).

Simple ruffles (hemmed or double thickness) make great 'collars' as well. Measure the neckline and multiply by the desired fullness factor to get the ruffle strip length.

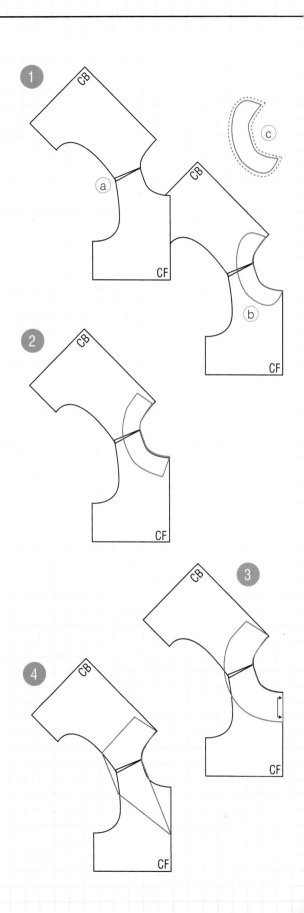

Sleeves

The sleeve blocks provided make classic puffed sleeves gathered at the top and bottom edges, and finished with a band at the sleeve opening. The band can be eliminated for a flared, hemmed sleeve. Other modifications include:

1. Less fullness – Move the centre line inwards by up to 2.5cm (1in) (a). Level out the bottom edge (b).

2. More fullness – Move the centre line outwards by up to 2.5cm (1in).

3. Cap sleeve – Raise the bottom edge at the centre line (a) and connect to the side edge with a curved line, at least 2cm (¾in) below the armhole (b).

4. Long sleeve – Lengthen the sleeve to three-quarter or full length (use the block and/or size charts as a guide). The bottom edge should be straight, and the band length should be adjusted as necessary.

5. Elasticised sleeve – Convert the seam allowance to a casing.

6. Flutter sleeve – Use only the top portion of the sleeve. For unlined bodices, you will need to create a facing for the armhole, as described on page 71.

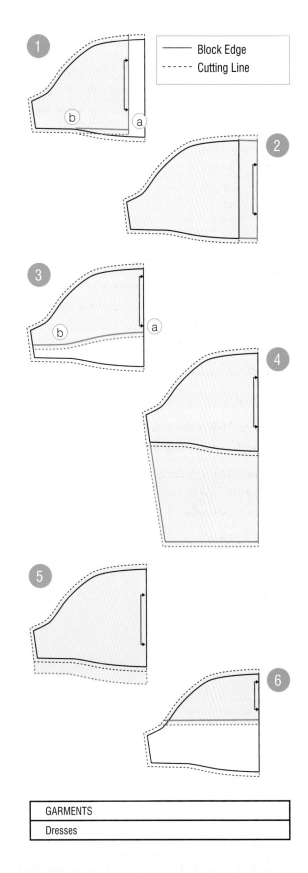

Clothing and photography: M&Co.

GARMENTS
Dresses

Facing and closure options

The bodice can be fully lined or finished with a facing (see page 20). For dresses with sleeves, only a neckline facing is needed.

Button or snap plackets

The basic bodice pattern includes 2cm- (¾in-) wide back overlaps and a folding allowance for a self-placket (1). For lined bodices, the fold allowance should be converted to a seam allowance (2). If the neckline is finished with a facing, it can be extended to include the placket, and the fold can be eliminated, as described in 2 (3). For a front opening bodice, the allowances should be eliminated from the back bodice and re-drawn on the front bodice (4).

Zips

If a zip is to be added, the cutting line should be placed 1.5cm (⅝in) from the centre back line (5).

Clothing: Andrea Thomas-Lambe of Thomas Parks Gifts.
Photography: Samantha Provenzano, Puddle of
Jumpers Photography.

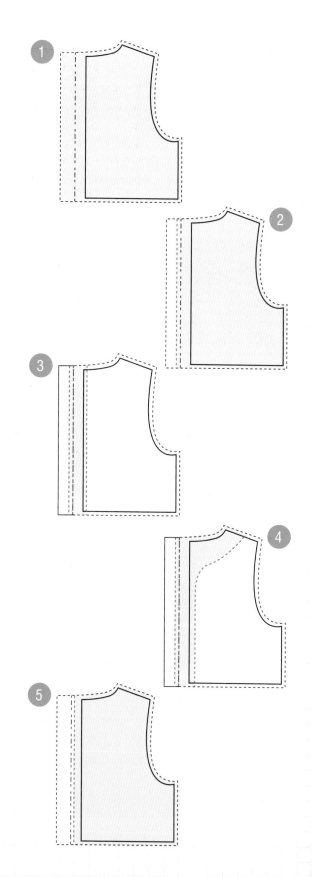

Extending fastener allowances into skirt pieces

Depending on the bodice length and fit, the opening may need to be extended down into the skirt piece. In general, bodices that are shorter than natural waist length should have an extension in the skirt to at least natural waist length level. Natural waist length bodices do not require an extension as long as they are wide enough at the base to slip over the hips easily.

Button placket extension

1. Full extension – The overlap and fold allowances can be added to the full length of the skirt so that it opens fully. Note: Since adding buttonholes and sewing on buttons is time-consuming, this is best reserved for shorter tops/dresses or those with a front button-up added as a design detail.

2. Self-placket – Extensions are added to the skirt piece so that when folded, they will be the size of the overlaps in the bodice pieces.

3. Attached placket – Similar to self-placket, but the extension pieces are separate, which conserves fabric and simplifies the cutting process.

4. Continuous bound placket – A single strip is used to finish the back opening, which can be a slit in the fabric or a seam.

5. For dresses with a zip, just include a 1.5cm (⅝in) seam allowance at the skirt seam that meets up with the bodice opening.

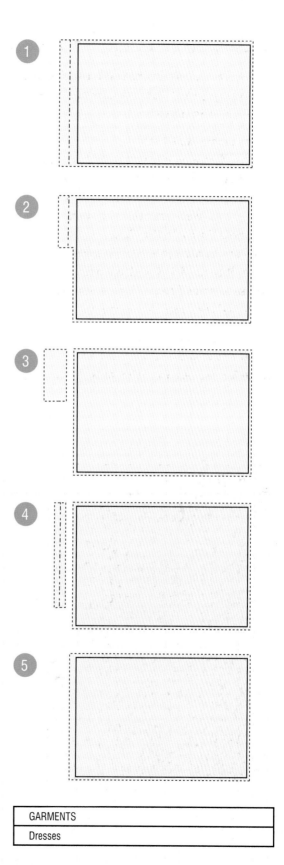

GARMENTS
Dresses

Yoke dress

The yoke dress is a sweet and youthful derivation of the basic bodice dress. It features a separate top piece that surrounds the neckline. The bodice is cut to accommodate the yoke piece. Fullness and length can be added to the bottom bodice piece to make a feminine, flowy dress.

To add a yoke to the basic bodice (1):
Align the front and back basic bodice dress blocks at the shoulder edges (a). Draw the desired yoke shape on the front and back bodice pieces, and eliminate the shoulder seam (b). Add the seam allowances to complete the yoke (c) and bodice piece (d) patterns. Note: The yoke is usually made from two identical pieces that are interfaced for stability. The bottom part of the bodice can be lined, or facings can be made to enclose the armhole edges.

To make a yoke dress with a full bottom bodice (2):
Draft the yoke as described above, up to step (c). Elongate the bottom bodice piece by the desired length, and make slash lines (d). Slash and spread to add fullness (e). Extend the back edges as needed to accommodate fasteners (see page 20).

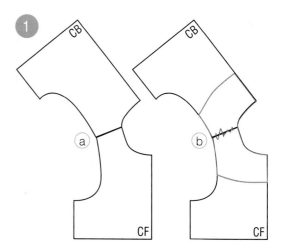

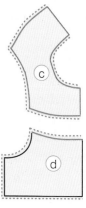

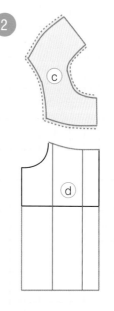

Clothing and photography: George at ASDA.

Other shape options include:

Square yoke (1)
Draft the yoke with lines parallel to the bottom bodice edges. Draw a square neckline in the front and the back. Extend the back edges as needed to accommodate fasteners. Note: The bottom edge of the yoke can fall near the bottom of the armholes, or closer to the neckline.

Bishop yoke (2)
Draft a circular yoke that extends beyond the edge at the shoulder point. Extend the back edges as necessary to accommodate fasteners. If you are adding sleeves, subtract the appropriate amount from the top of the sleeve pattern (a). Alternatively, you can create a flutter sleeve that does not fully encircle the armhole (b).

Round-neck yoke (3)
Draft as described for the bishop yoke, but add overlapping shoulder tabs and place both pieces on folds. Because of the opening at the shoulders, no other fasteners will be needed.

Mock-tuxedo yoke (4)
Draft as described for the bishop yoke, but make the yoke longer in the front (a). Draw a line to separate the centre front so that a different fabric may be used in the centre section (b), then cut (c). Embellish the finished product with ribbons, buttons and/or ruffles.

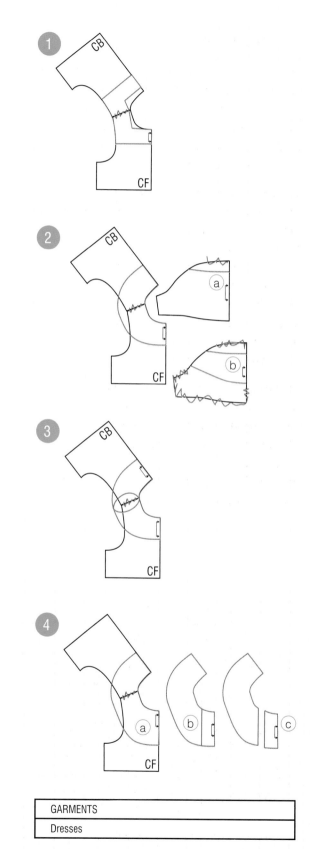

GARMENTS
Dresses

Jumpers

Jumpers are pull-on (or pull-over) dresses that have enough neck and arm opening space to forgo a zip or button placket. They can be worn alone, sundress-style or over another garment. The basic bodice pattern block may be used to draft a jumper dress. For fitted jumper dresses (1), use the existing side and armhole edges. For looser jumpers, to be worn as overdresses, drop the armholes by at least 0.5cm (¼in), and move the side line outwards by 0.5–1.2cm (¼–½in) (2). The bodice can be left at natural waist length or shortened into an empire length (3). Looser-fitting jumpers can be elongated into a dropped-waist style (4).

The bodice can be attached to a full skirt (gathered, pleated or circle), as described in Chapter 7 (5). Note: Since jumpers are pull-over styles, openings may be eliminated in the skirt pieces. Jumper bodices can also be elongated and expanded into more of a shift style (6). The garment should be wide enough at the bottom to easily slip over the head. Since the top part of the bodice is already open and/or free-fitting, add the fullness below the armhole position. Draw a horizontal line at the desired fullness start point, then slash and spread below this line.

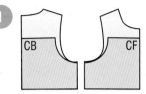

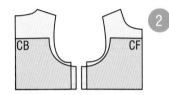

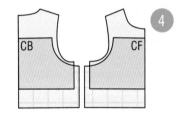

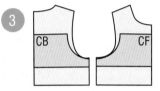

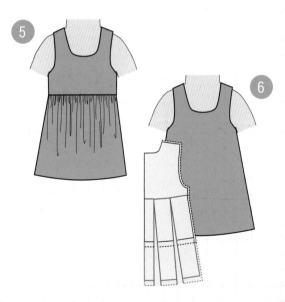

If the neckline is sufficiently wide – over 55cm (22in) in total – no fasteners are needed and the bodice pieces can be sewn together at the shoulder seams (1). Another option is to create bib-style front and back straps — draft as described on page 107, but shape as shown in (2). Separate straps may be used to connect the front and back bodice. For straight straps with no fastener, add in a slight curve so the straps hang properly on the shoulder (3). Tied straps are more flexible and can be made from strips of fabric (4). The 'knot' style fastener is also a popular option (5). Straps attached to the back are threaded through front buttonholes and secured with knots. A cute and very functional variation on the strap is the scrunched elasticised strap (6). The fabric 'tube' is made twice as long as the needed strap length. The elastic is cut to the needed length and inserted into the tube like a casing, which makes gathers.

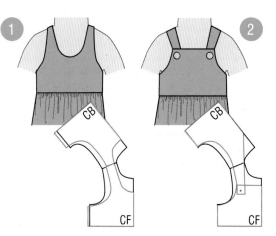

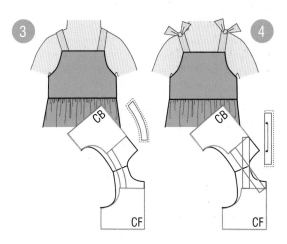

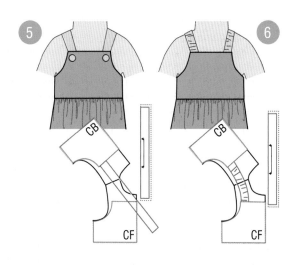

Clothing and photography: Littlewoods.

GARMENTS
Dresses

Clothing and photography: Breanne Crawford.

Chapter 9
Playsuits

The playsuit, or romper, combines a top and trousers into single-piece cuteness. Simple overalls are great for rough-and-tumble boys. Add ruffles to the leg openings and/or waistline for instant girliness. Knit overalls make great costumes and/or pyjamas. Easy-breezy pull-on playsuits can be made from the basic peasant pattern. Feminine sunsuits can be created by mixing halter or jumper tops and shorts or knicker bottoms.

Basic Playsuits

The playsuit, or romper, is a comfortable, one-piece wardrobe option. Any top style can be connected to trousers; it is just a matter of getting the right length and fit. The bodice block and the trouser block can be joined at the waist edge with the centre edges in line to make a playsuit block.

A basic playsuit block pattern is provided. It makes a playsuit that is semi-fitted in the chest area and roomier in the seat. The crotch is dropped slightly to allow for movement and comfort when sitting. This style is mostly worn by younger children (up to 5 or 6), but variations are popular for all sizes.

For girls, ruffles and flair can be added to the leg openings (see page 89). The puffed sleeves from the basic bodice dress may be used.

The playsuit can be lined or faced (see page 20). Allowances for a self-faced back placket with a 2cm (¾in) overlap are included but can be relocated to the front or modified for a separate placket/facing or a zip (see page 61). Alternatively, shoulder tabs may be added, as described on page 115.

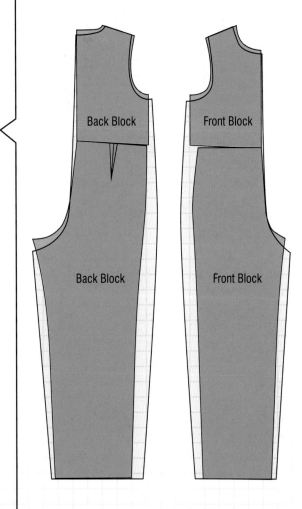

Basic playsuit block modifications

To eliminate the side seams and make a single pattern piece playsuit (1): Cut the front and back block at the side block edges and place the pieces together so they are touching at the hips. Connect the block and cutting lines.

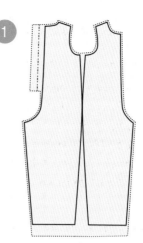

To make a playsuit with a semi-fitted bodice and full, gathered trousers (2): Draw a cut line (a) at the desired 'waistline' (empire, natural or dropped) on the front block piece. Separate the top and bottom pieces. Then add a bottom seam allowance to the top piece (b). Slash and spread the bottom trouser piece as described on pages 83–84 to add the desired amount of fullness (c). Add a top seam allowance to the bottom piece (d). Repeat for the back block piece.

To add blousing (3): Draw a cut line at the natural waistline (a). Cut and spread the pieces to add 2.5–5cm (1–2in) at the waistline (b). Connect the block and cutting lines (c). Mark the position of a casing or shirring (see page 49) underneath the bottom cut line (d).

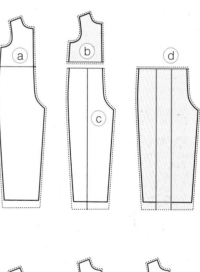

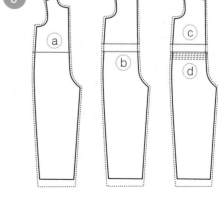

NOTE

The bodice block will overhang the trouser pattern a little at the side because it allows more ease in the waist area.

Opposite: Clothing: Taya Fisher of Ladybug Bend. Photography: Kari Forbush of Sweet Pickles Photography.

GARMENTS
Playsuits

Overalls and coveralls for all

Overalls are great for boys and girls, and can be made by reshaping the playsuit block. Use durable fabric to make utilitarian overalls for hard work and play. The T-shirt and playsuit blocks can be merged to make a knit coverall, or one-piece, with long or short sleeves. Use soft knits or fleece to make comfy loungewear or pyjamas.

Overalls (1)

Draw a V-shaped yoke with strap extension in the back (see page 77), and drop the armholes to just above natural waist length (a). On the front piece, draw a horizontal line at the same level as the armhole on the back piece (b). Draw a second line below the first to create the front waistband (c). Cut the pattern at the lines. Draw a bib shape on the top front piece and add seam allowances (d). Add seam allowances to the waistband piece (e). Add the top seam allowance to the bottom trouser piece (f).

Knit coveralls (2)

Place the T-shirt blocks over the playsuit blocks, aligning the neckline/shoulder corners. Use the shoulder, armhole and neckline edges of the T-shirt block, and the back and side edges of the playsuit block. Modify the T-shirt sleeve block as desired (see page 55). Note: For pyjamas, relocate the opening to the front (see page 81).

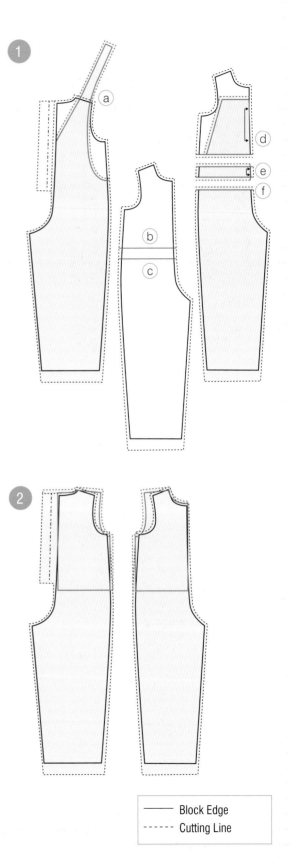

——	Block Edge
- - - - -	Cutting Line

Costume ideas

Overalls and coveralls make for warm, comfortable costumes. With all the available fabric options, the possibilities are endless.

Overalls:

Firefighter – Make the overalls out of black or brown canvas. Add reflective tape. Pair with a jacket (page 60) and firefighter helmet.

Construction worker – Use sturdy denim, and be sure to add lots of pockets (page 52) for holding tools. Do not forget the hard hat!

Train engineer – Use striped denim to make classic engineer overalls. Accent with a red bandana tied around the neck.

Coveralls:

Puppy/Cat/Bunny – Any number of animal costumes can be made with the coverall pattern. Use soft double-sided fleece or fun furry fleece in the desired colour. Add spots or belly accents, and of course a matching headpiece with the appropriate ears.

Clown – Mix and match fabrics, embellish with pom-pom 'buttons', and add a fun ruffled collar.

Dinosaur/Lizard – Add a stuffed tail to the back piece. Depending on the type of dinosaur, spikes can be sewn in as well.

Superhero – Recreate the bodysuit/underwear look by colour-blocking the coverall pattern (page 51). Do not forget the cape!

Opposite: Clothing and Photography: Penneys. **This page top:** Clothing and photography: Tu at Sainsbury's. **This page bottom:** Clothing and photography: M&Co.

GARMENTS
Playsuits

Playsuits and sunsuits for girls

All-girl playsuit variations are popular with both toddlers and tweens.

Pillowcase playsuits

For both the front and back playsuit block pieces: Redraw the neckline edge so that it extends from the outer shoulder corner to the centre line at the desired neckline level (a). Drop the armhole/side corners by about 1.2cm (½in), and position them 1.2cm (½in) beyond the side block edge (b). To add flare to the legs, drop the side line straight down at hip level (c). Eliminate the back opening (d). Relocate seam allowances. Optional – create a single-piece pattern and/or add blousing, as described on page 129.

Peasant playsuits

Modify as described for pillowcase playsuits, but use the peasant block as a guide for shaping the armhole edges. Modify the peasant sleeve pattern as desired.

Sunsuits are cool, breezy playsuit variations. They may be created by modifying the playsuit block to have a jumper top or by combining shorts and halter patterns.

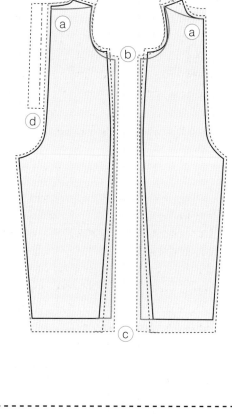

This page: Clothing: Taya Fisher of Ladybug Bend. Photography: Kari Forbush of Sweet Pickles Photography.
Opposite: Clothing and photography: River Island.

Jumper (1)

Modify the playsuit block to have a separate top and a full bottom, as shown on page 84 (a). Shape the top, as described on page 124. Note: The back opening may be eliminated if straps, ties or tabs are added at the shoulders. Adjust the length of the playsuit bottom to shorts length (b). Finish the bottom leg opening edge with a ruffle, cuff or a casing.

Halter (2)

Draft a natural waist-length halter bodice, as described on page 76 (a). Draft the desired shorts pattern, as described on page 92 (b). Note: For a full, gathered bottom with an elasticised back, draft single-pattern trousers (see page 88). For a more fitted sunsuit, draft shorts with a flat front and an elasticised back (see pages 82–83). Then overlay the shorts and halter patterns atop the connected bodice and trouser blocks to make sure the combined length gives the proper crotch depth (c). If needed, modify the shorts and/or halter patterns so the block edges meet at the desired position. If the side lines are at a similar position, the top and bottom pieces may be merged (d). Add allowances to the finished pieces (e).

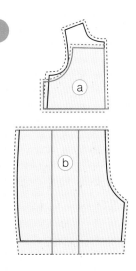

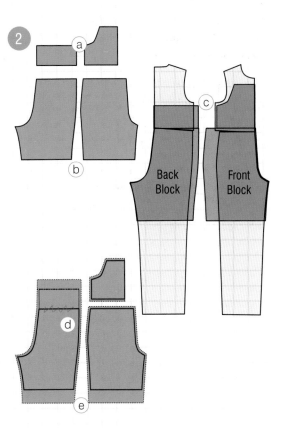

Back Block

Front Block

GARMENTS
Playsuits

This page: Clothing and photography: Woolworths. **Opposite:** Clothing: Jennifer Paganelli and Carla Hegeman Crim of Sis Boom. Photography: Annie Heng-Tse of Ella Sophie Photography.

Clothing and photography: M&Co.

Chapter 10
Taking it further

In the past, pattern production and distribution required access to specialised equipment and/or a big outlay of expense for printing and advertising. Now, one can affordably launch and market a pattern company with a home computer and internet access. Pattern-drafting software is available, but commercial versions (for making patterns to sell) are quite expensive and can be difficult to master. Most independent children's pattern designers use illustration software to draft, grade and tile PDF patterns. Adobe Illustrator is easily the most popular, feature-rich program, but free programs like Inkscape may also be used to make professional-quality patterns. As far as marketing goes, the internet provides so many great places to advertise your product. It is also a great space to network with potential customers and to gain feedback in the testing and development process.

Importing and digitising

You have drafted a great pattern and are ready to share it with the world. Or perhaps you are keeping the pattern for your own use and want to store it electronically. How do you get it from a large sheet of paper to a computer file that can be shared, printed and reassembled?

Scanning (1)

Unless you have access to a large-format scanner, you will need to break the pattern into bite-sized pieces for scanning. The portion size should be slightly smaller than your scanner bed, usually A4 size (8½ x 11¾ in). Using this box size, draw a grid over a copy of the full-sized pattern (a). Try to minimise the number of boxes to cut down on the number of scans. Depending on the thickness of the paper, the pattern can be folded or cut at the grid lines. For large patterns, number the pieces for future reference. When scanning, the piece should be centred on the scanner bed and backed with a dark piece of paper (b).

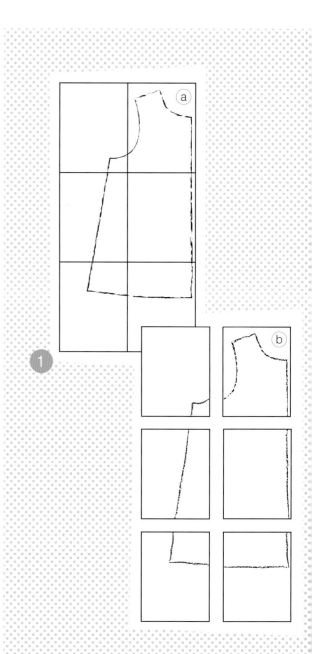

Stitching (2)

Save the scans as .jpg files and open them in your photo-editing software. If the scans are crooked, rotate the images to make them straight. Crop the images to the grid lines (clearly visible as the contrasting edge against the dark background). Note: Make sure the document size is close to that of the grid box. Make a new image file that is a bit larger than the total grid dimensions. Copy and paste each scan into the new image and arrange them like puzzle pieces, making sure the lines connect properly. Flatten the image.

Digitising (3)

The next step is to open the image in a program that has drawing capabilities. Some programs, like Adobe Illustrator, have automatic trace features that will convert your line drawing into an editable vector shape. If not, you can re-draw the shape over the scanned image, then delete the image. If the original pattern was neatly drawn it can be used as is, but be sure to erase any previous grid lines.

Tiling (4)

Draw a grid of boxes that are 19.5 x 26cm (7¾ x 10¼in) over the top of the pattern. There are two options. The first is to place the boxes side by side, and add reference marks for reassembly by butting and taping the pages together (a). The other is to overlap the boxes by 1.2cm (½in) so the pieces can be overlapped and taped or glued (b).

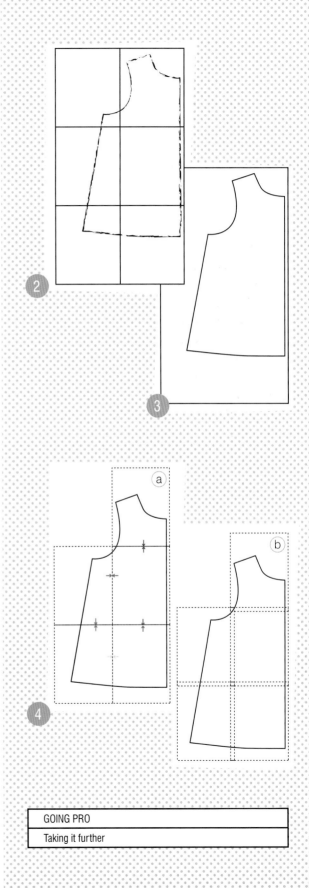

GOING PRO

Taking it further

Labelling (5)

The pieces should be assigned letters and/or numbers so they can be reassembled in a logical order (5). Assembly marks or overlaps should be labelled clearly to indicate the adjoining piece(s). At least one section should include the pattern name and size. Be sure to include all relevant markings needed to use the pattern as well (examples include grainline, fold placement and notches). In addition, a 2.5 or 5cm (1 or 2in) box should be added so that the end user can verify proper output size.

Transfer (6)

This is best accomplished by copying the sections individually and pasting them sequentially into the word processing or presentation software you are using to prepare your instructions (see page 142). Just be sure they are pasting at the proper size – 19.5 x 26cm (7¾ x 10¼in) – and centred on standard printer size individual pages, A4 (8½ x 11¾in). Once all the instructions and the patterns are complete, the file can either be saved or printed as a PDF. Note: It is helpful to include a page just before the pattern pages that explains how to print, instructions for measuring the test square, and a chart indicating which pages should be printed for individual sizes.

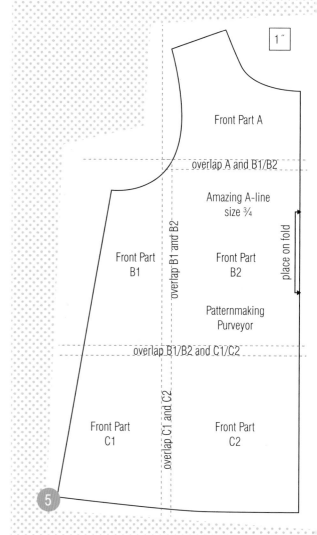

Grading (7)

If you are offering more than one size, you can either draft each size individually or use a process called grading to extrapolate multiple sizes from a single size. Since children's proportions change so much with age, it is best to use a combination of drafting and grading. For free-fitting styles, a ⁵⁄₆ can be graded down to a ³⁄₄ or graded up to a ⁷⁄₈. An ¹¹⁄₁₂ can be graded down to a ⁹⁄₁₀ and up to a ¹³⁄₁₄. For more fitted styles, a single numeric size should be drafted and scaled to no more than two numeric sizes in either direction. There are several methods of grading, and they can be accomplished on paper or digitally using illustration software. These methods are discussed in detail online and in grading textbooks (see page 150 for resources). Note: Automatic pattern grading software is available, but professional versions that can be used for commercial purposes are expensive).

Cut and spread grading: The pattern is cut at landmark points and spread apart (grading up) or overlapped (grading down). The spacing is based on the overall horizontal or vertical difference in sizes at that particular area, divided between the different sections.

Pattern shifting: The intact pattern piece is placed on a sheet of paper for tracing. Between edges, the pattern is shifted the distance needed to add or subtract the necessary height or girth.

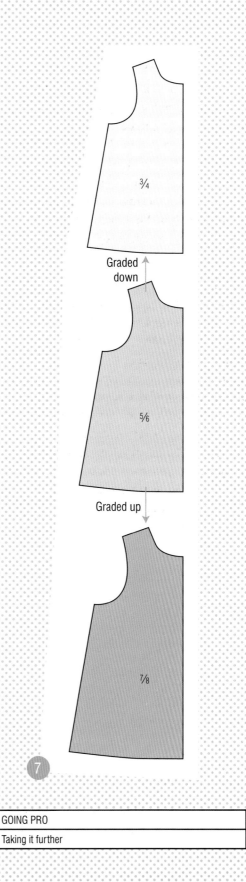

¾

Graded down

⅚

Graded up

⅞

7

GOING PRO

Taking it further

Writing instructions

So much goes into a complete pattern beyond pattern pieces.

Pattern description – Include a brief summary of the garment that will be made using the pattern. Also feature information about the fit, style and options available.

Sizing information – Provide the sizing information that is pertinent to the garment. If you are making a top, for example, the chest measurement range should be given for each size. It is also helpful to provide finished garment measurements.

Materials needed – List the tools that are needed beyond the basic sewing implements, such as glue sticks and marking pens. For fasteners, mention the size and/or quantity that is required. If elastics or trims are being added, provide yardage/meterage. For fabric, it is best to provide the quantity needed for each size (see cutting layout below).

Cutting layout – Lay out the pieces (either digitally or on paper) to determine the optimal placement for fabric cutting. Make a small graphic representation of where the pieces should be placed, leaving enough space to allow for user error or fabric shrinkage.

Terminology and techniques – Depending on the intended skill level, you may need to provide descriptions of or instructions for any technique that might be new to the end user. This is also a good place to provide links to additional internet resources.

Step-by-step sewing instructions – The beauty of PDF pattern distribution is that there are no page constraints for explaining how to construct the garment. This allows you to provide detailed descriptions and corresponding graphics. That said, do not waste page space (and the end user's ink/paper) with excessive white space or overly large fonts, photos or illustrations.

Numbering – You may find it helpful to number the steps. The pages should be numbered so they can be kept in order.

Text – This is your opportunity to give all the information necessary to complete a step. Relevant information (seam allowances, which sides are facing, what edge to stitch) should be included, and distinct steps should be separated with a space or two.

Artwork – Illustrations, photos or a combination of both can be used to show how the garment should look at each sewing stage. Illustrations can be drawn using illustration computer software or drawing tools contained within your word processing or presentation software. The beauty of illustrations is that they clearly show stitching positions. Digitised pattern pieces can be scaled down and used for the illustrations. Use an image of a print as a fill for a more realistic fabric look. Adjust brightness and contrast to make a faded version to represent the wrong size.

NOTE

Some people are visual learners, and others work better from descriptions. Try to provide as much information as possible in both the text and artwork.

Clothing: Andrea Thomas-Lambe of Thomas Parks Gifts. Photography by Samantha Provenzano of Puddle Jumpers Photography.

Photography

If you are using photography to explain construction steps, clear, concise images are a must.

Helpful hints

- Set up a work area with a simple background that will provide contrast against your materials.

- A medium resolution is sufficient to allow for cropping and editing. Keep in mind that image sizes should be relatively small (but still crystal clear) in the finished document.

- Use fabric that has a discernible right and wrong side. Also, sew with a thread colour that is visible against the fabric.

- Take your photos as you are writing your instructions (you will be far less likely to miss a step).

- For the sharpest pictures, use a tripod. If you need to show your hands in the shot, use the timer on the camera (and make sure you have clean fingernails!).

- Try to work in an area that has good natural light, but avoid harsh shadows. Also, do not use the flash unless absolutely necessary.

- It is a good idea to take multiple pictures of each step, making minor adjustments as you go. Be on the lookout for stray threads or other distractions.

- For small, detailed steps, zoom in accordingly, using the macro setting if needed. Use arrows and text as needed to point out details.

Sample photography

It is important to have photographs that are aesthetically pleasing and show off the fit and design of the garment. The main product image (considered the 'cover shot') should show the full garment on a child or a tailor's dummy. It is helpful to provide additional photographs for potential end users to see multiple views of the garment. If the pattern covers a range of sizes, consider showing multiple models. There are several means of obtaining great photos.

Take your own – If you have a co-operative child who is the right size, he or she can model. You do not need an overly expensive camera, as long as you have a good sense of colour and lighting. If possible, take the pictures outdoors, in a nice setting like a park. Try to take pictures under overcast skies or at dusk, when the shadows are not so harsh.

Use tester photos – Many willing testers are also talented photographers. Be sure to get a model release that allows you to use the photos for commercial purposes.

Hire a photographer – There are quite a few mummy/model teams that consist of a talented photographer and an adorable child. Many of them will exchange modelling services for item(s) being modelled. Others require a small fee, and some will do it for free as long as their watermark is included on promotional pictures.

Clothing: Andrea Thomas-Lambe of Thomas Parks Gifts. Photography: Samantha Provenzano of Puddle Jumpers Photography.

Testing

Tester feedback is essential to ensure the patterns give the correct fit and the instructions are understandable.

Finding testers – While you can ask close family and friends to review your work, it is usually best to get unbiased opinions from strangers. Social networking (which is critical for marketing, as described on page 148) is a wonderful means of finding testers. When you are first launching a line, you can put out tester calls on large sewing discussion groups. Facebook groups are a great place to connect with other seamstresses. If you are offering a multi-sized pattern, try to get each size tested (and it does not hurt to have more than one tester per size). Also, try to recruit testers with varying levels of sewing experience.

Expectations – Most designers give the patterns to the testers free of charge. Each tester, in turn, sews up the garment using his or her own materials within an agreed-upon time frame. Most testers will happily provide detailed feedback about fit, quality of instructions and general sewing experience (and like editors, they will find all of your typos, which is a good thing). Photographs are helpful for verifying fit and (if the tester is agreeable) may be used for marketing purposes.

Copyright considerations

As with most legal matters, there are lots of grey areas when it comes to the copyrighting of PDF patterns. Issues that come up include:

File sharing – Purchased PDF patterns are protected by the same laws that prevent the sharing or resale of downloaded songs, e-books, etc. that are not in the public domain. You should include a copyright statement to this effect.

Sale of resulting products – Some designers include copyright statements that prohibit the use of their patterns for making items for sale. Others offer licences (for a fee) that allow for limited sales. It is difficult to say whether these restrictions would be upheld in a court of law. From personal observations, it is generally in the best interests of the pattern-maker to allow small businesses to use patterns to make items to sell.

Intellectual property – If you have published a pattern, no one is allowed to reuse your text, photographs (step-by-steps or product images) or illustrations. They can, however, make an identical design and possibly use your pattern pieces. Therefore, your best bet is to keep your instructions top-notch and stay ahead of the game design-wise.

Opposite: Clothing: Andrea Thomas-Lambe of Thomas Parks Gifts. Photography: Samantha Provenzano of Puddle Jumpers Photography. **This page:** Clothing and photography: M&Co.

Distribution and marketing

Once your pattern is completed, you can sell it over and over again in a variety of places. In order to get maximum reward for your efforts, it is important to draw attention to your product through the magic of marketing.

Where to sell

Your own website – If you are tech savvy, you can design and/or maintain your own website to market and sell your patterns. You will need to be set up for e-commerce and have shopping cart, payment processing and (ideally) instant-download capabilities. You also need to make sure your site is 'seen' by search engines so that people can find it when they are looking for patterns. Much lies within the coding of the website itself, but links on other sites can also affect search-engine rankings.

Etsy – Etsy is a wonderful community of makers and customers who appreciate handmade products. It is a great platform for new designers to get seen and accumulate some feedback. The fees are low, downloads are instant and the listing process is simple. Payment processing is generally through PayPal, which is also inexpensive and user-friendly.

Craftsy – This social networking site has grown into an excellent marketplace for PDF pattern designers. There are no fees and it is a great opportunity for communication between designers and customers. Files are provided as instant downloads.

Third-party 'e-tailers' – Some sites offer PDF patterns from multiple designers. The more established sites have large mailing lists and can reach a wide audience. Smaller sites are more likely to support a handful of designers that fit with their design aesthetic. Generally, e-tailers will get a 50 per cent commission on sales. Before entering into an agreement with an e-tailer, get positive references from one or more of their existing designer partners.

Where to advertise

When selling an electronic product, the best form of advertising is also electronic. There are many affordable and effective ways for the PDF pattern designer to advertise:

Blogs – The best place for customers to get to know you and your product is on your own blog. You can come up with a multitude of posts about design inspiration, helpful tutorials and your creative life in general. This is also a great place to announce new releases, hold contests or advertise specials. You can also participate in other blogs, either by guest-posting or allowing a blogger to review your product. Advertising slots are available on well-read sewing/crafting blogs. Even better: submit original content as a feature (with a link back to your site).

Facebook – Facebook has numerous sewing groups, many of which allow the promotion of patterns. These are great places to advertise new products and promotions. You can also create fan pages and groups especially for your business. Fan pages are good for informational and advertising purposes, while groups allow you to network with customers in a more intimate setting.

Twitter, Pinterest and Instagram – These quick-sharing methods are gaining in popularity. The key is to gather a large, relevant group of followers and then stay on their newsfeed. Post interesting news bits or photographs frequently (but not excessively).

Clothing: Judy Buchanan of Hickity Pickity. Photography: Georgia Handy.

Resources

Further reading

Armstrong, Helen Joseph, *Patternmaking for Fashion Design* (Prentice Hall), 2009

Aldrich, Winifred, *Metric Pattern Cutting for Children's Wear and Babywear* (Wiley), 2009

Barnfield, Jo, *The Vintage Pattern Selector* (Barron's Educational Series), 2012

Barnfield, Jo, and Richards, Andrew, *The Pattern Making Primer* (Barron's Educational Series), 2012

British Standards Institution: www.bsigroup.co.uk

Consumer Product Safety information (US): www.cpsc.gov/en/Regulations-Laws--Standards/CPSIA/The-Consumer-Product-Safety-Improvement-Act/

Extended design services

Useful software
Adobe Illustrator
PC-compatible program for designing and drafting sewing patterns.

CorelDRAW Graphics Suite
Professional graphic design software for illustration and page layout, drawing and tracing tools, photo-editing and website design software.

Inkscape
An open source vector graphics editor, with capabilities similar to Illustrator, CorelDraw.

Microsoft Office
Suite of products that includes Word (word processing) and PowerPoint (presentation program with drawing tools that are great for layout, basic illustration and even pattern digitising).

Online tutorials

Threads Magazine – Making Sense of Pattern Grading: http://www.threadsmagazine.com/item/4368/making-sense-of-pattern-grading/page/all

Size charts

http://shop.bsigroup.com/ProductDetail/?pid=000000000019988653

Public domain size charts (US) can be found at:
http://gsi.nist.gov/global/docs/vps/psfiles/PS_36-70.pdf

http://gsi.nist.gov/global/docs/vps/psfiles/PS_54-72.pdf

This page and opposite: Clothing: Andrea Thomas-Lambe of Thomas Parks Gifts. Photography: Samantha Provenzano of Puddle Jumpers Photography.

Glossary

armhole: the arm opening that is either faced or attached to a sleeve in a finished garment. Also known as 'armscye'.

bell sleeve: a sleeve with a wide opening. The bell can be created with flare or a ruffle.

bias: a grain with natural stretch that runs diagonally, at 45 degrees, to the selvedge.

block: a basic pattern for a particular garment style, which includes both wearing and design ease. This can then be modified to create further patterns. Also known as a 'sloper'.

bodice: the part of a fitted garment that goes over the shoulders and around the front and back of the chest.

cap sleeve: a very short sleeve. Can be grown-on to the body by slightly extending the shoulder line, so that it 'caps' the shoulder, or can be 'set-in'.

casing: a folded or sewn-on section of fabric that encloses elastic or a drawstring.

colour blocking: a section of the garment is pieced using multiple fabrics to add design interest.

convertible collar: a collar that is worn folded so that the top edge meets or covers the neckline.

cut on fold: creates a mirrored piece from a half-section. Fold a section of fabric and place the pattern fold line on the fold.

darts: stitched sections, usually triangular or diamond-shaped, that take in areas of excess fabric and add shaping. In children's wear, they are usually seen in more formal clothing and larger sizes.

design ease or tolerance: is an amount of fullness given to a garment (beyond design ease) to achieve a more a particular look.

drafting: the creation of a block using measurements and calculations.

edge finishing: a stitching or cutting treatment that prevents fraying of raw edges on the inside of a garment.

empire waistline: a waistline that falls several centimetres above the natural waistline.

epaulette: a decorative shoulder piece found on military-style shirts and jackets.

extension: adding length to a pattern. Can be achieved by extending lines or by cutting, shifting and reconnecting the pattern.

facing: a shaped piece of fabric that is sewn to a garment opening to encase raw edges and add stability. A facing can be placed on the inside or the outside of a garment.

fit control: a treatment that brings the garment in closer to the body. Darts, shirring and casings are examples of fit control.

flat collar: a collar that sits flat around the shoulders.

flare: a portion of the garment that incrementally widens with length.

flounce: a circular element that is attached to a garment opening, giving the look of a ruffle without gathering.

flutter sleeve: a gathered sleeve that does not fully encircle the armhole.

frankenpattern: existing pattern pieces are merged together to create a new design.

fullness: extra fabric added to a pattern piece for shaping that can be used to flare, gather or ease.

gathering: an edge of the fabric is drawn together, either by pulling threads or using a specialised sewing machine feed.

grading: the practice of sizing a pattern piece up or down using set, incremental grade rules, or measurements.

grain: the thread direction of the fabric. It can run parallel or perpendicular to the selvedge edge of the fabric.

grainline: a straight line on the pattern piece that denotes the direction in which the pattern should lay, generally parallel to the selvedge edge.

hem: a folded or rolled finish to a garment edge. Single hems are edge finished and folded once, while double hems are folded twice to encase the raw edge.

hem allowance: the amount of length required to achieve the desired finished hem position.

interfacing: a supportive material that is either sewn or fused to the wrong side of a garment piece.

lining: an inner shell of the garment, made of a lighter-weight fabric, that encloses all of the internal seams.

mash-up: pattern pieces from different sources are recombined to achieve different garment options.

mirror-image piece: a symmetrical pattern piece, which, flipped on a mirror line, creates the complete garment section.

natural waistline: the bend point of the torso.

notches: small snips made in the seam allowance to mark where two garment pieces are to be matched and sewn together.

peek-a-boo: a layer of the garment is gathered or tacked to reveal an underlayer of fabric.

peplum: a short, decorative element attached to the waistline of a skirt or dress.

placement line: a pattern marking that gives positioning instructions for fabric cutting.

placket: a reinforced opening or slit in a garment. For garments with buttons or snaps, the placket edges overlap.

princess seam: a seam that runs through a bodice or skirt at the position of the dartline, adding fit control and visual interest.

raglan: a sleeve that has the shoulder sections of the back and front bodice merged, making a sleeve that extends diagonally from the base of the armhole to the neck.

ruffle: a gathered strip that is attached to the garment.

seam allowance: an extra amount, for example, 1cm (½in), added around the pattern to allow for garment pieces to be seamed together and properly finished.

selvedge: the self-finished edges of the fabric. Derived from 'self-edge'.

set-in sleeve: a sleeve that is sewn in to an armhole.

shirring: lines of stitching with elasticised bobbin thread on the underside of the garment.

size chart: a standardised guide of body measurements for each size. In children's clothing, sizes correspond to averages for different age groups.

standing collar: a collar that extends up and away from the neckline.

stretch: the ability of a fabric to be pulled in a given direction and recover. Knits can stretch in one or both directions relative to the grainline, while woven fabrics can only stretch slightly on the bias (45-degree angle).

tiering: strips of fabric are sewn together at the long edges, usually with gathering, to achieve the desired length.

toile: a test garment made from inexpensive fabric to verify and optimise fit. Also known as a 'muslin'.

upcycling: existing garments are cut and used as material for new creations. For example, adult-sized T-shirts can be used to make girls' dresses.

vent: a small, finished slit or opening in a bottom hem that allows for increased movement.

wearing ease or tolerance: the amount of fullness given beyond the basic body measurements to allow for movement and comfort.

yoke: a fitted top portion of a garment that is attached to a looser-fitting lower portion.

Clothing and photography: M&Co.

Index

Acknowledgements

Many thanks go out to:

The team at RotoVision, especially Isheeta Mustafi, for clear vision and dedication to this project.

Janice Pariat, for keeping the writing process fun and on track.

Fellow PDF pattern designers and enthusiasts for the inspiration and fellowship provided during the writing process.

Jennifer Paganelli, Cathy Peckiconis and Jeanine Thomlinson for keeping our pattern business thriving.

Much appreciation to my family for their love and encouragement. Thanks Mom, Dad, Delmar and Louis.